Herbert Hoover and Poland

HOOVER ARCHIVAL DOCUMENTARIES

General editor: *Milorad M. Drachkovitch*

The original documents reproduced in this series (unless other-wise indicated) are deposited in the archives of the Hoover Institution on War, Revolution and Peace at Stanford University. The purpose of their publication is to shed new light on some important events concerning the United States or the general history of the twentieth century.

Herbert Hoover and Poland

A Documentary History of a Friendship

compiled and with an introduction by
George J. Lerski

foreword by
Mark O. Hatfield
U.S. Senator, Oregon

HOOVER INSTITUTION PRESS · 1977
Stanford University   Stanford, California 94305

The Hoover Institution on War, Revolution and Peace, founded at Stanford University in 1919 by the late President Herbert Hoover, is an interdisciplinary research center for advanced study on domestic and international affairs in the twentieth century. The views expressed in its publications are entirely those of the authors and do not necessarily reflect the views of the staff, officers, or Board of Overseers of the Hoover Institution.

Permissions received and gratefully acknowledged for use of copyrighted material from Frank E. Mason, literary representative and agent of the Herbert Hoover Foundation, Inc., New York.

Materials from the Herbert Hoover Presidential Library, West Branch, Iowa, are reprinted courtesy of Thomas T. Thalken, Director.

Letters reprinted from *Organization of American Relief in Europe, 1918–1919,* edited by Suda Lorena Bane and Ralph Haswell Lutz, with the permission of the publishers, Stanford University Press. Copyright © 1971 by the Board of Trustees of the Leland Stanford Junior University.

Address "On the Food Situation in Poland" reprinted from *Addresses upon the American Road, 1945–1948* by Herbert Hoover, © 1949, courtesy of D. Van Nostrand Co.

Hoover Institution Publication 174

to Belva Jeanne

A free Poland is not dead. It will rise again . . .

HERBERT HOOVER
May 3, 1953

Contents

Foreword

In Warsaw, Poland, there was a square highlighted by a monument which bore the inscription, "Herbert Hoover." When dedicated in 1922, the dignitaries of Poland were joined by 100,000 school children, all who gathered to demonstrate their gratitude to the man who had saved hundreds of thousands from starvation and demonstrated the deepest humanitarian caring for the war-torn people of that land.

This is a chapter of American and Polish history which has lapsed from the contemporary memories of each of these nations. By reviving it, however, we may discover relevant wisdom for this present era.

The author, Professor George J. Lerski, is uniquely suited for this task. Not only is he a competent scholar of European history who has drawn upon the wealth of resources available at the Hoover Institution, but as a kindergarten student in Lwów, Poland, Lerski received meals given through Hoover's efforts in the early 1920s to save the children of Poland.

World War I had left much of Europe starving. Hoover's concern was manifest from the war's outset, as he led efforts to feed the starving in Belgium and other nations occupied by Germany, striving to overcome supposed military necessities, such as a blockade, with his humanitarian appeals. Hoover's concern for the Poles, however, could not be put into action until the Armistice was signed. But then he moved expeditiously, knowing that millions faced starvation before the harvest of 1919 would be available.

For the next three years, the American Relief Administration, under Hoover's leadership, provided half a billion meals to the hungry and starving of Poland. At the height of this operation, 1,315,490 Polish children were being fed each day.

Lerski tells this story with thoroughness and discernment, collecting documents published with the volume which yield the data of history to explicate Herbert Hoover's relationship with Poland.

The dramatic feeding of Poland's starving is only one aspect of this account. Hoover's relationship to Poland had major political consequences for that land as well, as Lerski explains. Particularly fascinating is the account of Hoover's relationship to the Polish pianist, and later Prime Minister, Paderewski. Professor Lerski demonstrates an understanding of the human aspects to history of diplomacy and politics as he traces Hoover's relationship with Poland through his election campaign, presidency, and then beyond in Hoover's later years.

When President Truman asked Hoover for his assistance in providing relief to Europe following World War II, a survey was made which concluded that only the United States, Canada, Australia, and Argentina had a surplus of food. As many as 1.8 billion people "were very seriously deficient in food supplies," and mass starvation threatened over 8,000,000.

An equally grave picture was presented to the World Food Conference in Rome twenty-eight years later, in November 1974. It estimated that by 1985, the countries of the world lacking sufficient food would need a staggering total of 85 million tons of food from nations with a surplus. Thus, the days when nations abundant with food are called upon to assist those people who face starvation still will mark our future, despite all the attempts undertaken to prevent such a troubling occurrence.

We would do well to recall the humanitarian spirit, administrative skill, and political wisdom which made Herbert Hoover beloved to millions throughout Europe whose bread came to depend during critical times on his compassionate character and commitment.

Appealing to the world's conscience, and particularly to Americans on behalf of the world's hungry after World War I, Hoover said, "The American people, in this most critical period of their history, have the opportunity to demonstrate not only their ability to assist in establishing peace on earth, but also their consecration, by self-denial, to the cause of suffering humanity." Such prophetic words, recorded in this volume by Professor Lerski, must be repeated to Americans this year and in the years to come, for they speak with the same truth and power now as they did then.

Hoover knew what we are only beginning to recognize today: that the right to food must be given the same priority in international politics as it demands in the lives of those who are starving.

Hoover demonstrated how foreign assistance can be justified on a clear humanitarian basis, given without demeaning the recipient, and utilized to nurture bonds between peoples that transcend political barriers. The publication of this book can help shed light on how that urgent task may be duplicated in our own time.

At the heart of Hoover's efforts was his resolute commitment to the plight of the oppressed—particularly to children. The Polish press described Hoover as "the broad-sighted American, friend of Poland, and above all, friend of those weakest, innocent victims of war—children." Would that we could profit from the witness of this international public servant by making that same commitment to those who this day have no bread to sustain their lives.

MARK O. HATFIELD
U.S. Senator, Oregon

Acknowledgments

The primary sources for this monograph were found in the two main collections of Hooveriana—in the Presidential Library, West Branch, Iowa, and, for the American Relief Administration period, the Hoover Institution on War, Revolution and Peace at Stanford, California. In searching for these materials and related clues, this author fortunately profited from the friendly, professional assistance of Mr. Thomas T. Thalken, the director of the Presidential Library; Mr. Robert S. Wood, the assistant director; and Mrs. Mildred Mather, its experienced archivist. At Stanford's Hoover Tower, Mrs. Crone C. Kernke and Mr. Ronald Bulatoff were very cooperative and knowledgeable in the archival research, while Mr. Charles Palm and Mrs. Dorothy Pond Morris were kind in providing logistic support. Ms. Ludmila Sidoroff was most helpful in the painstaking rechecking of the footnotes and Ms. Marty Zupan is responsible for her conscientious final editing.

For his scholarly assistance and patient advice, I am very grateful to my distinguished colleague, Dr. Milorad M. Drachkovitch, the archivist of the Hoover Institution. I am thankful to Professor Witold Sworakowski for his useful critical comments and for offering me important sources. Messrs. Richard T. Burress and Richard F. Staar deserve my gratitude for offering me a research grant, without which I could not have proceeded.

But most of all, I owe the completion of the manuscript in adverse circumstances to the stamina, editorial assistance, and typing of my wife—to whom this book is dedicated.

List of Documents

Introductory Essay

Introduction

For two centuries Poland and the United States have been friends. The present project was first conceived as a documentation of that friendship because of two events of the recent past: the Bicentennial of the Republic, and the centenary in 1974 of Herbert Hoover's birth. Throughout his public life the thirty-first president of the United States was more deeply involved in Polish affairs than any other occupant of the White House. Hoover's persistent idealism, tempered by a healthy pragmatism, produced significant relief in Poland after World War I. Parallel to his great humanitarian work for the welfare of Polish children was his unswerving political commitment to Poland's independence.

The attitude of the Poles toward their benefactor was cogently expressed by the American Minister in Poland, John B. Stetson, Jr., in a letter to President-Elect Hoover in November 1928: "Your name is second only to that of President Wilson in the minds of the Polish people. Their feeling for President Wilson is abstract; for you it is personal because of the tremendous services you rendered in supplying the population with food and other necessary articles immediately after the armistice."[1]

The author of this book in his early childhood in the 1920s was given "Hoover meals" in a Lwów kindergarten. But Hoover's involvement in Polish affairs started earlier and lasted much longer than his post-World War I philanthropic operation known as the American Relief Administration. Moreover, Hoover's attitude toward the Poles was just one example of his empathy for the "underdog"—Belgium, Finland, and Poland each became especially close to him. His particular interest in these three countries cannot be attributed merely to his Quaker background. A deep understanding of their respective historical predicaments and a lifelong personal interest in their contemporary problems played an almost equal role. In the case of Finland and Poland, he was also aware of the importance of "bulwarks against Bolshevism."

To illustrate the many facets of Herbert Hoover's involvement with Poland over several decades, the author has selected various documents and photographs that reveal Hoover's basic attitudes and significant activities.

The introductory essay puts the documents into their proper historical context and provides background materials that will, it is hoped, enhance the understanding and knowledge of the readers. The essay covers three essential periods in Hoover's relations with Poland: his post-World War I relief efforts, his attitude toward Poland as president of the United States, and his interest in Polish affairs as elderly statesman of the United States, especially following World War II.

Before proceeding with this narrative, however, it may be appropriate to relate the circumstances of Herbert Hoover's acquaintance in his early youth with one of the most illustrious Poles—Ignacy Paderewski. Hoover met the Polish virtuoso during his college years when the latter was touring the Pacific Coast. According to Hoover's own recollections of the event:

> With two other students at Stanford University, I conducted a small enter-tainment bureau which arranged for artists to come to the University for their usual fee. We sold tickets to the performance—by way of working our way through college. At a brave moment in our undertaking we engaged Mr. Paderewski to give a recital at the University. Unfortunately, some weeks later, on the date he was to appear, the University declared a holiday and I managed to set up the recital at the neighboring town of San Jose. But the inhabitants did not buy half enough tickets to cover our liability to the great pianist. When he arrived, we determined to confess to him our misery. We offered his manager all the money we had and promised the balance from future earnings. Paderewski took the incident as one of his humorous experiences and assured us that our payment discharged the debt.[2]

Perhaps the understanding that Paderewski showed for an embarrassed Stanford student contributed to Hoover's sympathy toward the artist's country in later years.

PART I

Relief during Armistice and Reconstruction

Hoover passed through Polish territory in 1913, but he first became seriously involved with Polish affairs in 1915. As chairman of the Commission for Relief in Belgium, he was approached by volunteer Polish organizations both in German-occupied Warsaw and in the United States to undertake assistance similar to that whereby food and clothing were provided to enemy-occupied northeastern France. Poland was suffering great devastation from the war and needed quick relief action. The first attempt to help the Poles came in November 1915 when Hoover, with German permission, sent his

senior associate, Dr. Vernon Kellogg, future secretary of state, to investigate
the gravity of the situation. Following Kellogg's grim report, Hoover tried
to make the proper arrangements with both belligerent camps. He first met
with representatives of the German General Staff and informed them that,
without a doubt, the Western Allies would set certain conditions before
allowing the International Commission for Relief in Poland, with its Berlin
headquarters under the neutral chairmanship of American Ambassador
James W. Gerard, to import the required food through the Continental
blockade. For instance, he believed that Paris and London would require
that Germany herself furnish "supplies equivalent to those which the German army absorbed in Poland."[3] When the Germans promised to cooperate
in the same way as they had with Hoover's relief action in Belgium, Hoover
wrote to Sir Edward Grey, the British foreign secretary, on December 22,
1915, with a formal proposal to help the Poles (Document 1).

Although he received a rather negative reply from Secretary Grey on
February 6, 1916, Hoover (with the cooperation of Frederick C. Walcott of
the Rockefeller Foundation) prepared a plan to feed four million people
in Polish cities (Document 2). U.S. Ambassador Walter Hines Page submitted the project to Grey on February 21, but protracted negotiations with
the Germans and the British bore no results. With the entrance of the United
States into the war, all chances for Hoover's intervention were vitiated.
Although a starving Poland was denied any substantial American help until
the Armistice, Hoover's relief negotiations contributed to an increased
political interest in that faraway country. As emphasized by the official
historians of the American Relief Administration, Harold Fisher and Sidney
Brooks:

> Sympathy for the war sufferings of the Poles merged with sympathy for
> their demand for the unity and independence of their nation. In this way the
> restoration of Poland became a war issue for a large public long before it was
> accepted by the foreign offices of Europe . . . popular support of Polish
> aspirations gained headway more rapidly in America than elsewhere, and
> this championship . . . was to be given new force in President Wilson's
> speech on January 22, 1917.[4]

Paderewski's subtle political activity and his close friendship with President
Wilson's top assistant in foreign affairs, Col. Edward D. House, brought the
Polish cause close to the inner council at the White House. As honorary
president of the Polish Central Relief Committee in the United States,
Paderewski was able to mobilize leaders of American Polonia. Their joint
effort was crowned by President Wilson's recognition of Poland's right to
independence with free access to the Baltic Sea, as worded in his famous
Thirteenth Point proclaimed on January 8, 1918.

The United States was the first world power officially committed to full implementation of the self-determination principle in East-Central Europe. By Armistice Day, November 11, 1918, all the Western Allies had one by one declared their support for Poland's full independence. With the return of Józef Piłsudski from German imprisonment, the first independent government was formed in the capital city to cope with the politically shaky and economically dangerous situation in Poland.

The chief executor of America's assistance to a reborn Poland was Herbert C. Hoover. Six days after the signing of the Armistice, Hoover sailed for Europe to organize mass food relief. Anticipating the relief needs of a famine-struck Europe, he had already begun preparations as food administrator for the United States.

> In the middle of October, 1918, when the Armistice was certain, we began to order extra quantities of food . . . and to fix a large number of ships for overseas transportation. . . . We loaded 58 or 59 cargoes before the end of November 1918 and a further 78 or 79 in December. In addition, I arranged for the use of some 250,000 tons of surplus army stocks and I borrowed some supplies from stocks of European neutrals against subsequent replacement. Before I left the United States for Europe (6 days after the Armistice) I arranged with the Treasury to make loans to cover food supplies during the acute period. . . .[5]

Hoover issued "An Appeal to World Conscience" on December 1, 1918, stressing that

> the people of Belgium, Northern France, Serbia, Roumania, Montenegro, Poland, Russia and Armenia rely upon America for immediate aid. . . . Upwards of 200 million people, in addition to those we are already pledged to serve, are now looking to us in their misery and famine. . . .

> The American people, in this most critical period of their history, have the opportunity to demonstrate not only their ability to assist in establishing peace on earth, but also their consecration, by self-denial, to the cause of suffering humanity.[6]

Upon Hoover's suggestion, a $100 million appropriation bill was passed by Congress on January 24, 1919. For the next three years Poland became a major recipient of generous and well-organized American aid that played a vital role in her postwar reconstruction.

Aware of Poland's urgent needs, Hoover chose to act even before official recognition of the newly established government, but he needed the cooperation of the Department of State. He decided to send Kellogg as a nutrition expert to study food conditions in Poland and on December 18, 1918, he asked Secretary of State Robert Lansing for authorization to delegate an American mission (Document 3). Facing procrastination by the European Allied governments, Hoover authorized Kellogg on December 23 to proceed to Poland with Col. William R. Grove who, as chief purchasing officer of the Quartermaster Corps in Paris, was detailed by the high command of the U.S. Army for service under Hoover. He asked Kellogg "to first determine the need of Poland and the method through which relief could be transported and distributed" (Document 4).

In addition to Kellogg and Grove, the mission was composed of Lt. Chauncey McCormick; Capt. Leo M. Czaja, M.D.; Alexander Znamiecki as secretary; Jan Horodyski as interpreter; and Sgt. J. Oliff from the Quartermaster Corps as "general utility man."[7] After stopping at Berne, Vienna, and Prague, they arrived in Poland on January 3, 1919, where enthusiastic crowds greeted them at railway stations despite bad winter weather.

When they reached Warsaw on January 4, Count Maurycy Zamoyski offered his Blue Palace as the first headquarters of the mission. Work began that same day with a series of conferences with Minister of Approvisation Antoni Minkiewicz and his staff and an official meeting with Józef Piłsudski, the chief of state. They "found him to be an agreeable man with a sense of humor. The discussion was informal. At this and subsequent meetings he was plainly dressed; no frills, no bunk."[8]

The missions's primary job was to ascertain what kind of assistance was needed and to get the food rolling as soon as possible without interfering in the domestic political problems of the new republic. This was in keeping with the policies of the entire European relief program. According to Colonel Barber, Hoover specified that all efforts were:

1. To help only those who could not help themselves.
2. To supervise only, taking no partisan interest in political or other problems.
3. To treat all nationalities and religions exactly alike.
4. To so organize the administration of every type of relief or advisory work that the native administrators would become increasingly efficient and ultimately take over the entire control.[9]

In his instructions to the food relief mission, the second point in particular was emphasized by "the Chief," as Hoover was called by his close associates. "Keep entirely out of politics. There are political missions assigned to political work, and we should forward to them any matters of interest in their work, or to the advantage of Poland in the general Allied cause, but your work is entirely that of relief."[10]

While his instructions to the mission were to concentrate exclusively on relief work, Hoover himself was involved in Polish domestic political affairs, especially in the Paderewski-Piłsudski conflict of January 1919.

Dr. Kellogg advised me of the impossible political situation. He felt there was only one hope and that was for Piłsudski, who had the army's backing, to be put on a pedestal. To close up the factions, he recommended that Ignacy Paderewski, the favorite of all Poles, should be placed at the head of a stronger cabinet as Prime Minister and take complete control of the civil government. . . . Dr. Kellogg asked that he be authorized to inform Piłsudski that unless this was done American co-operation and aid were futile. I did so and got the hint reinforced from President Wilson. As a result, Piłsudski was elevated to the position of "Chief of State," and Paderewski became Prime Minister on January 16.[11]

Hoover's admiration for the Polish artist may have been the main factor in his expressed preference for Paderewski as the head of government. Also, Piłsudski's past association with socialism, though it was the Polish type of intensely patriotic and democratic socialism, may have bothered Hoover, who throughout his life was a consistent opponent of any form of socialism. In spite of Hoover's political philosophy and his personal preference for Paderewski, he expressed high regard for Piłsudski also. In his August 15, 1919, address in Lwów, he said, "Poland is fortunate in having in her leadership two out of the six or seven great idealist statesmen of the world, Mr. Piłsudski and Mr. Paderewski."[12]

The United States was the first power to officially recognize the Polish government. On January 22 Secretary Lansing sent a cable to that effect to Prime Minister Paderewski. The American example was soon followed by other Allied countries.[13] America's role was no doubt one of the most important factors in Poland's regaining independence after World War I; Herbert Hoover played a substantial role in it second only to Woodrow Wilson.

Hugh Gibson, the first envoy in the history of Polish-American relations, was appointed by President Wilson on April 11. He had distinguished himself during the war as a diplomat closely associated with Hoover's Commission for Relief in Belgium. As "one of the outstanding products of nonpartisan professional diplomacy," commented his biographer, Gibson "stood ready to help point the way to rational, efficient, and democratic government in East Europe. . . . His adaptability qualified him well for such a post as Warsaw."[14]

Grove spent his first six weeks in Poland busily visiting the major cities, industrial centers, and remote areas particularly hit by famine. The original report of the Kellogg and Grove mission estimated that, out of some twenty-seven million people living early in 1919 under the control of the new Polish government, those to be saved from starvation before the availability of the 1919 crop numbered at least four million, and that ten million were in need of additional food to put them in condition for work.

This program required the importation of 348,250 metric tons consisting of 216,000 tons of flour; 72,000 tons of beans, peas and rice; 54,000 tons of fats; 2,400 tons of condensed milk and 3,850 tons of miscellaneous articles.[15]

Figures submitted by the Polish Ministry of Approvisation were generally accepted by the American Food Mission to Poland as a working basis for the initial relief needs.

The major problem facing the relief mission was that American food had to be delivered to the port of Gdańsk (Dantzig) at the mouth of Poland's main waterway, the Vistula River, and this required speedy implementation of the "free and secure access to the sea" clause of Wilson's Thirteenth Point. The eastern Germans, far from feeling defeated, were still quite reluctant to recognize Poland's rightful independence. Kellogg and Grove appealed to "the Chief" for proper supply arrangements via Gdańsk and the German railway to the Polish frontier. In his "Preliminary Report on Conditions in Poland," Kellogg wrote on January 6, 1919:

While the Poles seem to be in possession of Dantzig itself, and British and American War Ships are in the harbor, the country behind Dantzig up to Polish frontier is in hands of Germans and no movements of supplies or personnel between Poland and Dantzig can be made without definite arrangement of Armistice Commission. Such arrangements can be based on article 16 of Armistice Convention. I am enclosing statement officially made by Polish Government concerning the carrying off into German territory by German troops of several thousand cars loaded with grain. Of these part have been recaptured by Polish soldiers in German Poland but they feel unauthorized, or find it impossible to send them back to Poland. Cannot arrangement be made by Armistice Commission to have this grain returned immediately to Poland? This would afford a much needed relief pending arrival of supplies from America.[16]

In response to this report, Hoover requested the Allied Supreme Council of Supply and Relief to invoke article 16 of the Armistice, which gave the Allies the right to access to Polish territory via Gdańsk. The council, in turn, requested such permission from Supreme Allied Commander Marshal Ferdinand Foch (Document 5).

The day after signing the request to Foch, Hoover instructed Grove about investigating the situation on the spot in Gdańsk, where the first cargo was to arrive "in about one week" with the contemplated monthly relief, approximately 60,000 tons, designated for the Poles. Having received through Foch a

positive reaction "in principle," but with some reservations from the
Germans, Hoover cabled to General Andrews at Army General Headquarters
warning him against being too soft with German foot-dragging.

> I have no doubt that the Germans will raise every detailed difficulty they can
> in retarding this transmission of food from Dantzig to Warsaw, as is evidenced
> by their desire for Colonel Grove to communicate with them via the Com-
> mission at Spa. Such an arrangement would be hopeless. . . . They should
> be at once instructed that Colonel Grove is our representative in food trans-
> mission to Warsaw and anyone with whom he associates himself as assistants
> are our representatives and that the Germans should loyally cooperate with
> this group in securing the results demanded by General Foch. It would seem
> to me any failure on their part is a violation of their undertaking under the
> armistice.[17]

In the meantime, due to the emergency situations in the city of Lwów,
which was besieged by the Ukrainian Nationalist Army, and in the coal-
mining area of Dąbrowa Górnicza, a special milk-for-children shipment
came by rail from Switzerland during the first week of February. The first
three ships—among them the *Westward Ho,* with cargo financed jointly by
the Jewish Joint Distribution Committee and the Polish National Department
of America—arrived in Gdańsk on February 17 loaded with wheat flour.
When the first carload of flour arrived in Warsaw, a Polish member of the
mission, Jan Horodyski, commented that "America is the only nation that
has ever made a promise to Poland—and kept it."[18]

From that first arrival on February 17 "until July 31st, 1919, the Dantzig
organization unloaded eighty ships and forwarded to Poland substantially
the 300,000 tons of relief supplies. . . . Of this, about three-fourths was
transported to Poland in 16,000 freight cars, and the remaining one-fourth
in 550 barges on the Vistula River."[19]

In the meantime, Hoover was fighting British attempts to reduce the
European Allies' share in relief expenditures. Reacting to such suggestions
by Sir John Beale, chairman of the Inter-Allied Food Council Committee of
Representatives, Hoover said: "I do not feel that I am justified in placing
before the liberated governments these arbitrary reductions. It is to me a
serious matter that the Council should fail to provide the supplies necessary
to give adequate relief against suffering to these liberated countries and to
promote their political stability."[20] That same day, February 3, 1919, Grove
was appointed by Hoover to represent the United States on the Allied
Commission for Poland. In the appointment letter Hoover specified arrangements to be made for revictualing the country.

In view of the delays caused by mounting British, Italian, and French
objections, the United States had to undertake the major part of the relief

work. On February 24, an executive order created the American Relief Administration (A.R.A.), under Hoover's directorship, and authorized its expenditure of $5 million to employ the U.S. Grain Corporation for the purchase and transportation of supplies from American to European ports. The Appropriation Act of February 25 enabled Hoover to secure vital food credits for Poland, since the A.R.A. could now accept 800 million marks from the Polish Treasury. Happy with this turn of events, Hoover decided to cable Prime Minister Paderewski that the uninterrupted stream of food supplies from the United States would continue to increase in volume. His telegram ended with a warm message: "It is now four years since I first attempted in cooperation with yourself to secure the international organization of systematic relief to Poland, and, late as the day is and as great as the suffering of the Polish people has been, yet I witness this day with no little personal satisfaction."[21]

By the end of the month the A.R.A. and the governments of Poland, Czechoslovakia, Romania, and Serbia had signed bilateral agreements in which mutual obligations were specifically stipulated. On March 11, following up on these agreements, Hoover sent official letters to the heads of the liberated states recommending the organization of national relief commissions to take over the A.R.A.'s operations "as rapidly as the development of the commission permits their absorption. There will thus be no interruption of the progress from economic illness to convalescence."[22] Concerned about the urgent need for assistance to the starving children, on March 17 Hoover sent Grove detailed instructions about convincing the Polish government to establish a Children's Relief Committee in every main industrial city (Document 6).

The explosive Gdańsk situation took a turn for the worse at the end of March, just as it seemed that the port would be able to handle the steadily increasing flow of American food and clothing. Fearing that Gen. Józef Haller's army (composed mainly of Polish-American volunteers) would seize the predominantly German city while passing from France to Poland, the German government proposed to the Allied Supreme Command that Haller's divisions be rerouted through other south Baltic ports—Szczecin (then Stettin) and Königsberg. To protect the smooth relief operation via Gdańsk, Libawa, and Kłajpeda (then Memel), and to avoid trouble between the Germans and the Polish troops, Hoover made the following proposal in a letter to President Wilson on April 2:

> I have been for many days filled with the greatest anxiety over the feeding of Poland, due to the proposed transportation of troops through Dantzig, the absorption of railway facilities, and the conviction on the part of all of our

staff that bloodshed and disturbances will break out, probably requiring considerable military occupation. . . . I learn, however, today, from General Bliss, that the Germans show a disposition to transport these troops overland direct from France. I cannot urge upon you too strongly the importance of taking this action and leaving the port of Dantzig alone to the food people until its fate has been decided by peace negotiations.[23]

In the spring of 1919, private American organizations (such as the Red Cross, Quakers, the YWCA, the Jewish Joint Distribution Committee, and the Polish-American Relief Organization) sent their own personnel to help the Polish and the Jewish populations. Hoover made successful attempts to coordinate their manifold activities through the A.R.A., which acted as a sort of transport agency for most of them throughout 1919.

His strong belief in private initiative led him to appeal to Americans of European descent for support of the feeding of children in liberated countries. In his April 25 cable to the New York A.R.A. headquarters, he urged:

We should use every opportunity to lay before the American people the tremendous volume of service that the United States is giving in Europe in this connection, as already nearly one million under-nourished children are being specially fed. What we do need is that you should amalgamate former bodies or create out of important nationals committees for each of the countries of Finland, Poland, Roumania, Austria, Czecho-Slovakia.[24]

The coal shortage in devastated Europe also came under Hoover's relief activities. In his efforts to assist in the economic reconstruction of Europe, Hoover could not remain passive when border quarrels over national minorities interfered with his general scheme. Obviously annoyed with the Czech-Polish controversy over the ethnically mixed Cieszyn area and eager to stimulate coal production in that region, he proposed a compromise solution in his communication of April 28 with Secretary of State Lansing (Document 7).

At the beginning of 1919, Poland produced only forty percent of her own normal coal requirements. Upon Hoover's recommendation, the Supreme Economic Council passed the following authorization on April 28:

The Director-General of Relief is charged for the present with all matters in connection with the endeavor to increase coal production and with the supervision of the distribution of the coal so produced in the former Empire of Austria-Hungary and in Poland working through the Missions of the Communications Section charged with the operation of the through railroad services for the distribution of food supplies in this territory.[25]

Acting on this authority, Hoover sent Col. Anson C. Goodyear of the U.S. Army as the president of a special "Coal Commission of the Supreme Economic Council for the territory included in the former Empire of Austria-Hungary and Poland." Usually referred to as the Allied Coal Commission, it was headquartered at Moravska Ostrava in Czechoslovakia, near the Silesian coal mines. The duties of the commission, composed of twenty-two specialists (twenty-one of them American), were "to effect an increase in the production of coal, and to arrange for a proper distribution of the coal produced" among the successor states of the former Habsburg Empire and Poland.

Sending copies of introductory letters to the various governments whose countries were to be covered by Goodyear's commission, Hoover wrote to the latter:

> The importance of this work you are about to undertake cannot be over-estimated from the standpoint of the re-establishment of order. The supply of coal to the railroads and the water communications is naturally of primary importance to this end. However, only secondarily in importance to the opening of the railways and water ways is the question of supplying coal to the factories and shops, engaged in work of an economic advantage to the general situation, and wherein existing idle labor may be put back into useful production.[26]

A grant of $100,000 was set aside by Hoover as a special gift of the American people to the undernourished children of the miners. Food purchased with this fund "produced almost as remarkable effects on the miners as on their children."[27] Another significant operation in the mining areas was Americans' donation of used clothing, which was distributed in Karwina, Katowice, and Dąbrowa Górnicza. According to Goodyear's report, this particular distribution "not only produced a favorable result in improving the living conditions of the miners and their families, but also established good relations from the first between the miners and the members of the Coal Commission."[28]

Though the Coal Commission had no legal authority to enforce or cancel any contracts, "it was Hoover's belief that as a disinterested, non-political body with the prestige of America . . . the Commission would be able to break through the national blockades and revive the movement of international trade."[29] Like Wilson, he was not sufficiently aware of the intensity of nationalistic conflicts in the area and thus believed also that the presence of the A.R.A. in the very heart of Europe would act as a catalyst for an economic confederation. He even wrote to that effect to Wilson on June 24, 1919, the eve of the latter's departure from Europe (Document 8).

With the acute antagonism between the Germans and Poles in anticipation of the forthcoming plebiscite, Hoover's expectations of intergovernmental arrangements for coal distribution in East-Central Europe were not fulfilled. Just as Goodyear was to finalize negotiations for a mutually advantageous Polish-German exchange of 10,000 tons of Poznań potatoes for 20,000 tons of Upper Silesian coal, the First Silesian Uprising against the German occupation broke out on August 17. Upon Hoover's request, Goodyear intervened between the belligerents. He accused the German authorities of an "act of bad faith" in delivering an ultimatum to the Poles. In view of the deteriorating situation and the expiration of the Coal Commission's mandate, Goodyear suggested that the Allied Supreme Command send an inter-Allied commission to help keep peace in Upper Silesia (Górny Śląsk) until the plebiscite. Such a commission arrived promptly at the beginning of September, with Goodyear as one of its four senior members.[30] Its work was hampered, however, by the successive uprisings of the Polish miners against the Germans.

The disorganized postwar transportation in East-Central Europe had to be dealt with as a precondition for any major food relief operation. Again the problem was within the purview of Hoover's numerous official functions.

American experts became involved as middlemen between the Poles and the Germans in the recurring problem of A.R.A. shipments from Gdańsk. As recorded by Fisher and Brooks:

> The Poles refused to allow their barges to enter German territory for fear of confiscation, and the Germans refused to send their barges into Poland for fear of injury to the barge personnel. Ryan [Maj. Thomas R. Ryan, an engineer in the U.S. Army] finally had the barges moving, after securing guarantees from the Polish War Ministry and from the Germans in Berlin through the A.R.A. Mission there. The rail shipments from Danzig were made under the agreement negotiated by Major Webb, of the A.R.A. Food Mission, whereby the Poles were to deliver 250 empty cars per day at the frontier to replace the German cars loaded with relief supplies.[31]

The tense situation required daily American intervention. Firmness, but also patience, was necessary to secure the steady movement of supplies.

Major Ryan assisted in restoring telegraph communications inside the country and between Warsaw and Vienna. After careful statistical research, he also helped the Poles in securing their claims to the German rolling stock turned over to the Allies with the Armistice. As repayment for the railway stock taken by the Germans during the wartime occupation and upon their withdrawal, 100 locomotives and 2,000 freight cars were assigned to Poland. This acquisition was of tremendous value to the Polish economy in view of a serious shortage of rolling stock and the appalling state of the existing engines and freight cars.

The Allied blockade of the territories occupied by the Central Powers hurt Poland since it continued until the peace treaty was signed. Admitted as "a friendly state" to the Paris Conference, Poland had to wait until the Versailles Treaty for the supplies handled by Hoover as general director of relief. By then her industries were at a great disadvantage because of the war devastation and the lack of credit or business connections. It was thus of great importance when Hoover could write to Paderewski on May 6 that "additional financing has been provided, which enables us to make a substantial start in the shipment of cotton in order that the Polish mills may be brought into early employment."[32] With American money, Hoover was able to purchase 25,000 bales of cotton to secure jobs for 250,000 of the unemployed textile workers in Łódź.

Gradually Hoover became involved in other Polish problems, including the sensitive one of Polish-Jewish relations. Polish lands had been a "haven of refuge" for the Jewish masses expelled from western European countries in the late Middle Ages. More Jews lived within the Polish-Lithuanian Commonwealth prior to the eighteenth century than in all the rest of the world. Under royal legal protection, they could maintain the autonomy granted to them in the Four Land Council system.[33] Relations between the Poles and Jews started to deteriorate during the last two decades of the nineteenth century under the impact of Russian pogroms and German racism. Polish anti-Semitism thereafter thrived primarily on economic competition between the late-developing Polish middle class and the entrenched Jewish bourgeoisie. Moreover, Poland of 1918 had to cope with some two million predominantly poor, Yiddish-speaking, and unassimilated Jews. Tragic pogroms were carried on in the eastern cities of Pińsk, Mińsk, Wilno, and Lwów during the first restless months of regained freedom.

World Jewry reacted with understandable anger. On May 21 American newspapers carried advertisements "in which it was stated that Jews were being slaughtered in Poland . . . and that the Jewish people had never been set upon by an enemy more merciless, more brutal, more determined, or more powerful." As explained by Fisher and Brooks, this was one instance of a general phenomenon. "Accounts of these affairs quickly spread abroad, greatly exaggerated, until it was widely believed that the new Polish government had organized pogroms against the Jews."[34]

Gibson, the U.S. envoy to Poland, kept reporting that "there was no evidence extant to sustain or verify allegations of widespread 'massacres' and that there was no organized anti-Semitic movement" in Poland. He maintained that, "to the extent pogroms against the Jews did exist in Poland, the

causes were more social and economic than religious." After visiting with
Boris D. Bogen, who had been in Poland since February as a representative
of the Jewish Joint Distribution Committee, Gibson reported to Washington
that as far as the eastern cities were concerned "Polish hostility toward Jews
had resulted from a popular belief that they were allies of the Bolsheviks
and that the Jews had been responsible for attacks on Polish troops." He
appealed to Acting Secretary of State Frank Polk for the State Department
to "discourage anti-Polish agitation" and prepare Jewish visitors to Poland
"to face the facts honestly and work patiently for the good of their coreli-
gionists." He recommended in the same communication that passports be
refused to "agitators of any sort, Jewish or Christian."[35]

To help in the tense situation, Hoover prompted Paderewski to write
directly to President Wilson with a request for the appointment of "an independent committee to investigate on the ground, to report its finding, on
the basis of which the Polish government should take proper action, and to
advise the Jewish community in Poland in regard to its relations with and
interest in the new democracy."[36] Hoover then wrote to Wilson supporting
the prime minister's request: an investigation would "give the Polish Government an opportunity to prove its good faith" in facing the hostile propaganda
from various quarters (Document 9).

Wilson responded in the affirmative and appointed a commission consisting of Henry Morgenthau, Brig. Gen. Edgar Jadwin, and Homer H. Johnson.
They spent two months in Poland, and on October 3 Morgenthau concluded:

> Just as the Jews would resent being condemned as a race for the action of
> their undesirable coreligionists, so it would be correspondingly unfair to
> condemn the Polish nation as a whole for the violence committed by uncon-
> trolled troops or local mobs. These excesses were apparently not premeditated,
> for if they had been part of a preconceived plan, the number of victims would
> have run into the thousands instead of amounting to about 280. It is believed
> that these excesses were the result of a widespread anti-Semitic prejudice
> aggravated by the belief that the Jewish inhabitants were politically hostile
> to the Polish State.[37]

The two other commissioners, in their conclusions of October 31, blamed
both sides: "Some representatives of the Jewish national movement who
have been conspicuously active refuse to subordinate the Jewish question
to the general need of the Polish State." On the other hand, they added, the
National Democratic Party had been involved in anti-Semitic propaganda.
While deploring the fatal incidents, which were "aggravated by intoxication
due to the looting of liquor stores, with usual adjuncts of criminal irresponsi-
bility and mob rage," Jadwin and Johnson expressed the belief that "none
of these excesses were instigated or approved by any responsible govern-

mental authority, civil or military." They praised Poland's acceptance of the minorities clause of the Treaty of Versailles "guaranteeing to all citizens security of life and property and equal protection of the laws." Far from whitewashing all the Poles for criminal cases of violence, they stressed that the Jews were not beyond reproach either:

> We find . . . that the history and the attitude of the Jews, complicated by abnormal economic and political conditions produced by the war, have fed the flame of anti-Semitism at a critical moment. It is believed, however, that the gradual amelioration of conditions during the last 11 months gives great promise for the future of the Polish Republic as a stable democracy.[38]

Years of war and the mass movement of refugees and armies across Poland caused the westward spread of typhus from postrevolutionary Russia. The Supreme Economic Council referred the matter to its own Food Section and, once again, to Hoover. Since the Allied governments failed to furnish the funds for these new tasks of the International Red Cross, Hoover initiated major action in Poland with the cooperation of the Polish minister of public health, Dr. Tomasz Janiszewski. In June 1919, stressing that "it becomes of vital interest that the whole world support the Polish Government to enable them to combat the disease," Hoover asked Judge Edwin W. Parker of the U.S. Liquidation Board in Paris for cooperation. Hoover endorsed Janiszewski's request for supplies and material from army stocks and indicated that Wilson was very anxious that Janiszewski receive all possible assistance. In the same letter Hoover undertook to support this urgent type of relief from his A.R.A. funds.[39] Included in the material obtained by the Polish government from the U.S. Liquidation Commission were "800 motorized vehicles, 1,000 steam disinfecting plants, 40,000 beds, complete, 10,000 clipping machines, 1,500,000 suits of underclothing, 30 mobile laundries, 250 tons of soap, and 5,000 portable bathing plants." In addition, Hoover agreed to make "the cost of transportation a gift from the A.R.A., representing its contribution to the typhus campaign."[40]

With Wilson's approval, Hoover subsequently asked General Pershing to detail Col. Harry L. Gilchrist of the Army Medical Corps to head the Polish Typhus Mission (Document 10). To speed up the matter in Washington, Hoover cabled Secretary of War Newton D. Baker on July 11 (Document 11). After receiving Baker's cable of authorization, General Pershing ordered Gilchrist on July 17 to report to Hoover. The expenses of the 18 officers and 500 enlisted specialists detailed to the anti-typhus campaign in Poland were paid by the United States.[41]

Colonel Gilchrist's mission involving bathing, delousing, disinfecting, and quarantine operations, proved to be invaluable, and the Polish authorities requested that Hoover extend its services beyond the originally planned four months. Secretary Baker notified Hoover on November 5 that the request had been granted, and Gilchrist remained in Poland throughout 1920. Conditions were pathetic, as indicated by excerpts from Gilchrist's report of March 1920:

> Houses have been visited by me in which the entire families were stricken, some delirious and without medical attention of any kind. . . . If the dead have no near relatives to claim their effects, the bodies are stripped before burial and their clothing taken away in ignorance by the peasants to distant parts to be sold, thus implanting the disease in new areas.

> There is a great dearth of doctors in some districts, there being but one doctor to each one hundred and fifty thousand inhabitants. . . . These doctors are doing a magnificent work, but are greatly overworked and labor under terrible handicap. . . . The death rate among doctors has been very heavy. . . .[42]

Following American advice, on July 24, 1920, the Sejm (Diet) passed an emergency law giving the epidemic commissioner, Professor E. Godlewski (Gilchrist's mission cooperated closely with him), extraordinary powers and full authority to act all over Poland.

The indefatigable Hoover also turned to the problem of prisoners of war. Not only did some half a million foreign prisoners pass through Poland, but there were about a million Polish subjects awaiting repatriation. As director general of relief, Hoover submitted a memorandum on July 26, 1919, to the Council of Five (France, Great Britain, Italy, Japan, and the United States) about the repatriation of prisoners of war, with some ideas on Allied funding for this huge undertaking (Document 12).

Without a doubt, however, the major concern to Hoover the humanitarian was the starving children of Poland (Document 13). The first program for the Polish children's relief was arranged by Colonel Grove and his associates by the end of April 1919; from the first special shipment, food was served in Brest Litovsk on the last day of April "to a hungry group of 2,000 children who thronged the first [American] kitchen in Poland."[43]

The primary target of the A.R.A.'s Children's Relief Fund was to efficiently organize a mission to Poland with the original assignment of $800,000 which was increased by the end of May to $2.4 million and matched by the Polish government. Prime Minister Paderewski met with the A.R.A. representatives, Colonel Grove and Lt. Maurice Pate, on March 22 to discuss the feeding of the children. The internal distribution and administration had been entrusted to the Polish Central Children's Relief Committee (Centralny Komitet

Pomocy Dzieciom), chaired by Mrs. Paderewska (wife of the premier). In June it changed its name to State Children's Relief Committee (Państwowy Komitet Pomocy Dzieciom), and in January of the following year it was renamed the Polish-American Children's Relief Committee (Polsko-Amerykański Komitet Pomocy Dzieciom), better known under the initials P.A.K.P.D. For several crucial years it played an important role in the extensive children's relief work in Poland.

American relief action for Polish children was established with two principal goals suggested by Hoover: "First, to provide during the period of emergency one meal per day for the neediest children and second, to develop from the native organization thus established a permanent institution which might function in the future as a country-wide child welfare organization."[44] Fundamental conditions of A.R.A. distribution were:

> (1) that foodstuffs be distributed only to the neediest children in Poland without regard to religion, nationality, politics or any other factor except the physical condition of the child; (2) that each child and nursing mother should have the right to receive one ration of food daily; and (3) that rations be served in prepared form and be eaten by children and nursing mothers at the kitchen.[45]

In addition to arrangements for the importation and distribution of foodstuffs and other materials, a system of supervision was devised. Each American representative was assigned to a certain territory to keep in touch with the local committees and employees and to instruct them about "fundamental principles of the action and the point of view of the American donors."[46]

The fact that 125,000 children in the neediest sections of the country were fed in May 1919 produced a great psychological relief. But it was not until June that A.R.A. operations were fully organized, with preliminary surveys conducted and local committees formed under the staff of Grove and Pate. As told by Fisher and Brooks: "Wherever the Americans went they found appalling signs of malnutrition among the children."[47]

The meals were systematically scheduled for six school days: Monday—rice with milk, sugar and bread; Tuesday—rice, pea soup, cocoa and bread; Wednesday—dumplings with bacon; Thursday—soup with beans and noodles; Friday—cocoa and a double ration of bread; Saturday—dumplings with beans.[48]

On July 3, prior to his departure from Poland, Grove prepared a detailed report on the relief provided to children. Hoover wrote to him with praise for "the exceptionally able and loyal services rendered" and sent laudatory letters of appreciation for Grove's efficiency and dedication to his superiors, Secretary of War Baker and Generals Pershing and Rogers.[49]

In view of the continuing need to feed children in Poland and despite Hoover's heavy duties in Paris, President Wilson asked him to "take his place" and visit the country to assess the gravity of the situation.[50] Hoover's triumphant visit marked the emotional apex of his involvement in Polish affairs. Hoover's own vivid description of his arrival in Warsaw on August 12, 1919, refutes allegations that he was devoid of a sense of humor.

> The platforms were lined with soldiers with massed bands playing "The Star-Spangled Banner"—and they continued to play it. We Americans lined up alongside of our train with our silk hats clasped to our bosoms if we were civilians or our right hands frozen to our caps if we were military. The Polish officials were likewise lined up with Piłsudski, Paderewski . . . likewise all frozen to salute in honor of the American national anthem. But the bands did not seem disposed to allow the salute to thaw out.

> Finally, after a year of embarrassing minutes, the Mayor stepped forward and presented me with the traditional Polish welcome of bread and salt. This time it was a round loaf of bread, eighteen inches in diameter, with a great salt crystal in the dome and all of it upon a specially carved wooden platter. . . . He spoke English but I could not hear a word. With my right hand frozen to the silk hat at my breast, I took the platter in my left hand with appropriate remarks which he in turn could not hear because the band played on. Quickly my left wrist began to wobble under the weight, and I just managed to pass it over to the left hand of the Admiral. His arm quickly began to wobble and he passed it to the left hand of the General. And I watched it go all down the line to the last doughboy. The Poles applauded this maneuver as a characteristic and appropriate American ceremony.[51]

The next day Hoover started his busy schedule with a press conference and a series of meetings with government officials, including Chief of State Piłsudski. That evening Prime Minister Paderewski gave a gala dinner in Hoover's honor, and Hoover delivered a speech emphasizing the preconditions for the economic reconstruction of Poland and vibrantly appealing for a true liberalism to ward off reactionism and extreme radicalism (Document 14).

August 14 proved to be the most memorable day of his visit. In the late afternoon some 32,000 Polish children paraded across Mokotów field in the heart of Warsaw. In Hoover's words, "The most profoundly touching incident was my reception at Warsaw by the children." Vernon Kellogg, who had reported to him in January that "we see very few children playing in the streets," was there with Hoover and Prime Minister and Mrs. Paderewski to watch the march, two and a half hours long, in front of the grandstand.

> They came with the very tin cups and pannikins from which they had just had their special meal of the day . . . thanks to the charity of America, as

organized and directed by Hoover, and they carried their little paper napkins, stamped with the flag of the United States, which they could wave over their heads. . . . These thousands of restored children marched . . . in happy, never ending files past the grand stand where sat the man who had saved them. . . . They marched and marched and cheered and cheered. . . . And all went by as decorously and in as orderly a fashion as many thousands of happy, cheering children could be expected to, until suddenly from the grass an astonished rabbit leaped out and started down the track. And then five thousand of these children broke the ranks and dashed madly after him, shouting and laughing. And they caught him and brought him in triumph as a gift to their guest. But they were astonished to see as they gave him their gift, that this great strong man did just what you or I or any other human sort of human being could not have helped doing under like circumstances. They saw him cry. . . . But the children of Warsaw had no need to be sorry for him. For he cried because he was glad.[52]

Hoover tells the same story in his *Memoirs,* adding that the head of the French Military Mission stood nearby "with tears coursing down his face until finally, overcome, he left the stand. He said in parting, 'There has never been a review of honor in all history which I would prefer for myself to that which has been given you today!' "[53]

Next, Hoover was bound for the beleaguered Lwów. Aware of the complex nationality problems in that fervently patriotic city, he decided to deliver an optimistic speech on behalf of the emerging Polish democracy (Document 15). He was greeted by another parade of children and warmly received by the Lwów population and its press.[54] Hoover spent several days in the region, even visiting the nearby front.

Hoover's train reached Kraków on August 17. The city council had issued special huge posters welcoming their American benefactor. Hoover visited the Kościuszko Tomb at the ancient Wawel Castle, where he addressed the crowd. "My speech was only about ten minutes long, as there were not a hundred out of the 30,000 massed people who understood English. After Paderewski had given about forty-five minutes to the translation, I asked my Polish aide what he was talking about. He replied, 'Oh, he is making a *real* speech.'"[55]

Even with the pleasantries and gala performances, this was one of Hoover's busiest days in Poland, as evidenced by the number of letters he wrote. Asked for advice by Paderewski, Hoover suggested the creation of an Economic Council to facilitate relief. He recommended that its purpose be "not administrative, but . . . for study, advice, and co-ordination of the administrative functions" of various governmental departments, and that "its scope should cover the entire domestic, economic and foreign problems of Poland." Comprised of "representatives appointed by the Ministers of Finance, Approvisation, Railways, Agriculture, Commerce and Industry,

Interior and Labor," it should be chaired by a "new Minister (without port-folio) to be called something like the Minister of Economics." Anticipating the need for some economic planning in Poland, Hoover expressed his belief that such council "would be at once accepted abroad as evidence of sound political and economic organization, and would be helpful in establishing that atmosphere of credit which we all so much desire for the new-born Polish Republic."[56]

Following up on those recommendations, the Polish government formed an Economic Council of Ministers with the finance minister as chairman. American technical and food advisers who went to Warsaw that summer were frequently consulted on such matters as taxation, loans, and currency. The most important of the advisers were Col. Alvin Barton Barber, who replaced Colonel Grove as head of the A.R.A.'s Polish mission, and E. Dana Durand.

Concerned about the lateness of the Polish harvest and the critical situation in the Lwów region which was devastated by the Ukrainian-Polish hostili-ties, Hoover wrote to Durand about the much-needed land reform:

> The whole impression that I got out of this trip is the complete necessity to undertake the agricultural problem at once. Nor do I get the impression that the smaller proportions of the land which must be divided to the peasants during the forthcoming year itself comprises any great danger to production, when you consider that probably four fifths of the proprietor's land in Galicia is not under cultivation even now. From a political point of view, if Poland wishes to hold the Ruthenians quiet, the quicker they give them the division of these estates the better.[57]

Convinced that Poland would need further American assistance, Hoover wrote to Gibson asking him to organize and chair a coordination committee of all American charitable activities in Poland. "A statement from this Com-mittee as to the necessities of Poland will have a great weight in the United States and I am anxious indeed that it should be proceeded with at any early moment, as I shall have to identify myself *in Poland's necessities for a long time to come.*"[58]

As soon as he returned to America, Hoover started to campaign through-out the country for understanding of Poland's needs in order to survive the next winter. Addressing the prestigious Commonwealth Club in San Fran-cisco in mid-October, he chose Poland to illustrate the situation in postwar Europe and commented: "Poland has more points of sentimental relations to the United States than any of the [other new states]. We have in the United States not only three millions of Poles but we have traditions in relation to

Poland not far behind those of France."[59] Outlining Poland's plight and emphasizing that it required moral and economic help from the United States, he ended his speech with an anti-isolationist appeal.

Aware of the strong ties of American Poles with their old country, Hoover addressed the All-Polish Convention at the Dom Polski (Polish Home) in Buffalo, New York, on November 12. He appealed for support of his relief operations in Poland, stressing the civic duties of Americans of Polish descent toward the new country (Document 16).

The operations for feeding children appealed to the young American women of Polish origin. The idea of mobilizing them was conceived in 1919 by Laura de G. Turczynowicz, whose Polish Reconstruction Association asked for the cooperation of the YWCA. She made a $1,000 contribution toward that goal and "urged that Polish girls in America should be given training which would fit them for reconstruction services in Poland." Because of the color of their uniforms, the women organized under this program were called the Gray Samaritans. Of some 500 volunteers, 300 young ladies took courses through the cooperation of physicians in Cleveland, Detroit, Milwaukee, Rochester, and St. Louis, and 90 of them qualified for scholarships in the Polish Gray Samaritan School, which opened in New York in October 1919. Although 75 of them graduated eight months later, only 40 saw service in Poland. Hoover, as head of the A.R.A., "warmly endorsed the plan to bring a unit of Gray Samaritans to Warsaw."[60] The first unit sailed on July 31. According to Barber:

> These girls, young and unspoiled, combined in a remarkable way the emotional enthusiasm and devotion of the Pole with the efficiency and persistence of the American. . . . They aided tremendously in the feeding program undertaken under Hoover, especially as department inspectors since they spoke both English and Polish. Carrying out the Hoover policy of self-help, fifteen of these girls took on as understudies fifteen young Polish college girls so that when the Gray Samaritan must finally return to America, there would remain in Poland a body of trained workers of practical experience in child welfare work.[61]

Hoover praised the Gray Samaritans on numerous occasions. An example is his letter to A. Lawrence Lowell, president of Harvard University, in which he singled out the Gray Samaritans as the best possible recipient of Lowell's $1,000 contribution for Polish assistance.[62] In 1922 Secretary of Commerce Hoover wrote a message of appreciation, "To the Girls of the Gray Samaritan Unit of the Y.W.C.A." In the letter, read at a luncheon held in their honor at the Bankers Club in New York City, Hoover expressed "the gratitude we all owe and the appreciation we hold for the extraordinary

services of the Gray Samaritans in Poland. The hardships they have under-
gone, the courage and resource they have shown in sheer human service is
a beautiful monument to American womanhood."[63] The girls of what was
later referred to as the first American Peace Corps received individual
letters of gratitude from Secretary Hoover (Document 17).

Hoover was alarmed by reports about the Bolshevik drive westward in
Europe. W. Parmer Fuller, Jr., the new chief of the Children's Fund Mission
to Poland, wrote on January 22, 1920, asking for "the Chief's" intervention.

> It appears that if Allied aid fails, the Polish Government is confronted with
> the two alternatives of making peace with the Bolsheviks or of being beaten
> by them. Without generous aid of materials the Government feels that it
> will be unable successfully to resist the Bolshevik offensive which is now
> confidently expected for late winter or early spring. . . . While the Govern-
> ment believes it has enough men it knows that it must have munitions, food
> and clothing from outside sources, and for these it cannot pay cash. . . .
> While April 1st is looked at as a likely date for the beginning of the campaign,
> this date also looms up as the beginning of general famine unless American
> flour arrives. . . .

In the same communication, Fuller stated that without Allied assistance the
Poles would be defeated by the Bolsheviks and that the results might "well
be widespread." Aware of local inefficiency, he implored in the names of
Barber and Durand that distribution of the additonal 300,000 tons of U.S.
flour be supervised by Americans. "In affording American supervision the
Chief would be doing one more favor to the Polish people."[64]

Hoover apparently had been impressed during his visit by the accomplishments of the Polish state and thus had confidence in its democracy. In
view of the 1919 experience with the Hungarian Soviet Republic and the
revolutionary tide in Germany, he was convinced of the crucial geopolitical
role of Poland. He expressed this view, and his faith in the Poles, in a speech
published in the April 1920 issue of the *National Review*.

> Poland to-day must hold the frontline of Europe against Bolshevik invasion.
> In the midst of her economic misery she must maintain an army of five
> hundred thousand men, fighting on a front of fifteen hundred miles, as the
> outpost of Europe. Yet the people of Poland are fired by an emotion of
> freedom that will carry her over another year of suffering.[65]

After Germany's collapse, East-Central Europe was in danger of a Bolshevik invasion. Lenin and Trotsky invited all the neighboring peoples of
Europe to join the Soviet Union; to implement such a policy, the Red Army

advanced in the footsteps of the disintegrating German troops. The main drive of this military operation early in 1919 was directed across Poland to support the revolutionary movement in Germany. In view of the civil war ravaging Russia, it was difficult for the Allies to settle the ethnically complicated problems of the Polish-Russian border. Led by Piłsudski, who proposed a federalist anti-Soviet solution of Lithuanian, Byelorussian, and Ukrainian problems, the Poles advanced eastward. In the spring of 1920, after the failure of armistice negotiations between Poland and Soviet Russia, the Poles attacked to help their Ukrainian and Baltic allies to regain independence. On May 8 Kiev fell to the Poles and Ukrainians. The overextension of the Polish offensive, however, enabled the Russians to regain the initiative and launch a major counteroffensive, which reached ethnic Poland in mid-July 1920.

Alarmed by the possible consequences of a Soviet invasion, Hoover cabled via London on July 14 the following tentative instructions: "It would be fine thing if some of our men would remain with Poles and continue to carry on Child feeding. . . . I don't know of any service that they could perform that would be finer. . . . They should of course send all American women and children out before such invasion."[66] Hoover's concern about the continuation of relief operations was well founded, as recorded in the work of Surface and Bland:

> The Bolshevist offensive against Poland . . . imposed a severe strain on the field organization of the child-relief work. During the invasion it was necessary to evacuate the relief supplies in advance of the Bolshevist army. . . . In August, 1920, when the final attack . . . was repulsed, 6 of the 11 regional warehouses, 6 of the 15 regional offices, and 93 of the 207 district offices were in the hands of the invading army. Due to the heroic work of both Polish and American members of the relief organization, the loss of child-feeding supplies was negligible. However, the occupation of nearly one-half of Poland and the wanton destruction of food and other supplies set back the reconstruction work in Poland by nearly a year's time. This made it necessary for the relief organization to redouble its efforts in the winter of 1920–1921, and introduced the further problem of caring for Russian and Polish refugees.[67]

Similar problems were noted by Colonel Barber: "Hundreds of thousands of refugees fled westward before the invading forces. The feeding of the population, the feeding of the children, the operation of the railway lines, the many other branches of the technical administration laid on them an almost impossible burden."[68] In spite of such difficulties, Hoover's food and technical assistance probably contributed more to Piłsudski's victory than the much-publicized French Military Mission under General Weygand.

The victory, as pointed out by Barber, brought new relief problems. With the Polish counterattack, "the overwhelming of the Russian army, their retreat which the Polish onslaught developed into a rout, and then again more problems of feeding the children in the newly devastated war areas, the spread of typhus, due to the refugees from Russia, the problems of reconstruction were again to be faced."[69] The wartime prime minister of the Government of National Unity, Wincenty Witos, decided to appeal to Hoover for American help in healing the many deep wounds of the war. He wrote on October 29:

> Our regenerated Motherland has received from you so many proofs of exceptional sympathy and owes you . . . so very much that now, when on account of events, Poland is facing again great difficulties . . . you will, Dear Sir, kindly consider this new appeal to you. . . .
>
> The invasion of the Bolshevik Army has thrown us back to the previous tragic situation. In an area of over half of the country crops were taken from the fields, grains from the barns, cattle were driven wholesale back to Russia or slaughtered to feed the Soviet troops, agricultural implements were destroyed. . . . We are doing everything in order to get out of this economic abyss. . . .
>
> Without a new action on broadest scale, . . . comprising a system of daily meals effected with that extraordinary efficiency and accuracy which always were the signs of your great work, one and a half million Polish children will be exposed to the danger of not being able to endure the winter. . . . We again look towards the great American people and you, the author of the largest work of Christian help planned and operated up to date.[70]

Hoover knew from the daily reports of his representatives in Poland about the new emergency needs and had acted accordingly. In the *A.R.A. Bulletin* of October 1 he strongly appealed to private and religious institutions and proposed an extension of the A.R.A.'s activities through the coming winter until the 1921 summer harvest. For there was "the continued necessity to feed approximately 2,250,000 in Austria, Czechoslovakia, Poland, Baltic States and other parts of Central and Eastern Europe. These are largely waifs and the children of destitute." He explained that, due to the cooperation of local authorities and charitable institutions, the estimated cost of "providing sufficient food, suitably prepared for a child per month is about $3.00 of which the outlay of the American Administration is about $1.00. Under this system, a comparatively small personnel has been required, and the total overhead cost of maintaining some 3 million children has not exceeded one half percent of the money expended." Although proud of the efficiency and frugality of his outfit, Hoover wanted the public to realize that "the American Relief Administration for this work will be exhausted by the first of January. It will require $20,000,000 for us to carry over the children needing help until the next harvest." Hoover concluded with an appeal for more financial effort and better cooperation.

> The primary feeding of these children . . . is fundamental to their survival, and must become a priority claim on all American sympathy and charity if a catastrophe of the first order is to be avoided. Conferences are in progress between the American Relief Administration, the Red Cross, the Jewish Joint Distribution Committee, the American Friends Service Committee, the Y.W.C.A. and the various church organizations, with a view to joint and cooperative action in the effective organization of American charity to meet the piteous call of these helpless children. . . .[71]

Under Hoover's auspices, these American organizations cooperated and worked very smoothly for the well-being of the Polish majority and national minorities.

Hoover's efforts were greatly appreciated in Poland. He was notified in October 1920 that he had been unanimously elected honorary president of the Polish-American Children's Relief Committee (P.A.K.P.D.) in "recognition and heartfelt appreciation of the immense service" which he had "rendered the needy children of Poland." In accepting the honor, Hoover once again spelled out his objective of American aid. "It has always been my earnest hope that, when American support of children's relief operations finally comes to an end, the citizens of Poland would see to it that the work of child welfare went on. I rejoice to know that such progressive and practical steps in that direction have already been taken."[72]

In the meantime, the relief work of the A.R.A. was getting publicity in the Polish press. The *Kurjer Lwowski* commented on October 30,1920:

> In the chaos of Diet speeches, war communiqués etc. not everybody knows of the existence of Polish-American Children's Relief Committee, whose aim is to bring aid to the neediest, underfed . . . Polish children regardless of creed and nationality. To create such an organization, two things are necessary: great, noble heart full of pure love for humanity, and a great devotion for children and understanding of the fact that these children are our future.

> The first man who brought relief to our country oppressed by war, the first man who put this important action on a real basis, was Herbert Hoover, the broad-spirited American, friend of Poland, and above all friend of those weakest, innocent victims of war,—children.[73]

Typical of the Polish appreciation of Hoover's ingenuity is the account given in *Robotnik* (Workman), the Warsaw weekly organ of the Polish Socialist party, of a unique Hoover charity banquet at the Commodore Hotel in New York.

It was served on wooden tables, pewter plates, without napkins, and consisted of potatoes, rice made with water and a cup of cocoa. It cost $1000 for one person. In the centre of an immense table stood a high chair for an absent child, and to this chair was fastened a candle which burned and threw some light on the evening dresses and white shirts of the banqueters. It was a symbol. The chair represented an absent "host" — a child — a hungry European child — and the burning candle the charity which irradiated the fate of the child. . . . Round him sat the richest men in the United States. . . . During this evening Hoover collected 1,000,000 dollars.[74]

Hoover received numerous accolades from the Polish people. Honorary doctorates were given to him by the University of Kraków (medicine) in 1919, the University of Warsaw (law) in 1921, and University of Lwów (law) in 1922. At a public meeting of the city council on November 10, 1921, the capital of Poland offered Hoover the title of honorary citizen of Warsaw. The town council of Lwów unanimously voted to give Hoover honorary citizenship during his August 1919 visit. That diploma was offered in his absence to William N. Gwynn, a representative of the A.R.A., in a special ceremony on June 21, 1921.

Touching in its simplicity was the 1920 Christmas cable sent from Chief of State Piłsudski on behalf of the children:

From the depths of our hearts we are sending thanks to you and our friends in America. The gifts of the American people to our children are the more valuable because they represent voluntary offers of countless American households. Today our children rejoice that they eat their Christmas dinner not as a mere stranger but as the absent guest of a million American homes.[75]

Particularly dear to Hoover's heart were the greetings from the children themselves. There are hundreds of them available in the A.R.A. Archives. One of his gifts was an album containing "over one million signatures of grateful Polish children."[76] He pointedly responded on December 8, 1921 (Document 18). Another example of Secretary Hoover's warm replies is his letter addressed to the children of Kutno, in 1922. "I was highly honored by your letter and poem which I have received with the picture which you have presented to me. I am indeed grateful and shall always treasure most carefully these expressions of your friendship."[77]

An appropriate expression of Polish gratitude occurred later, in 1927, when Polish school children heard about the Mississippi Valley floods. They "collected nearly $2000 which they sent through the Polish-American Society at Warsaw to Mr. Hoover for the relief of juvenile flood victims."[78]

Flattery on the part of officialdom did not affect Hoover's sober grasp of Polish shortcomings, however. With his acquired knowledge of Polish affairs, and being critical of bureaucratic inefficiency or financial incompetence, on February 2, 1921, he temporarily declined to appeal to the American public for charity for food relief (Document 19).

The Poles' handling of finances, discussed by Hoover, was to be a recurring problem. In February 1922 Durand, who served under Hoover in the Department of Commerce as chief of the Eastern European Division, wrote to Secretary Hoover giving his comments on the Polish obligation to the United States. Apparently the State Department was "seeking full information regarding Polish finances." Durand felt that the weekly report of Trade Commissioner Smith dealing with the "extremely delicate . . . and difficult to handle" question of liquidating this particular debt deserved Hoover's personal consideration. Anticipating trouble, Durand transmitted Smith's warning that

> Unless due regard is given to the actual ability of countries such as Poland to pay interest and principal . . . misunderstandings will surely arise and American prestige and trade will suffer. I do not by any means intend to convey the idea of cancellation but would strongly urge the Bureau to interest itself in this matter to the extent of endeavoring to bring about the adoption of a formula which will give full consideration to the effect of funding operations on American Trade in the future. This subject carries a bigger load of explosive material than the matter of tariff legislation.[79]

The accomplishments of American relief operations in Poland between 1919 and 1921 were many and multifaceted. It was "largely on Hoover's recommendation [that] the United States Government released to Poland credit for food, engineering and other supplies which finally amounted to $159,666,972" at $4\frac{1}{4}$ percent interest.[80] Although the A.R.A.'s food program reached its peak in May 1920 with 1,315,490 children fed daily, throughout the first half of 1921 the figures again surpassed one million persons daily fed at 7,650 stations throughout Poland (Documents 20, 21).

According to an article published in the Warsaw daily *Rzeczpospolita* (Commonwealth) on July 4, 1921, the value of the food and clothing distributed in Poland through Hoover's child-feeding program was around $35 million.

> The total amount of foodstuffs distributed to the children of Poland up to June 1st, 1921, is approximately ninety five thousand tons (95,000 tons). This represents some 9,500 freight cars, which if joined together would make a train over 42 miles long. The number of meals distributed since the beginning of the action to June 1st, 1921 is five hundred fifty million (550,000,000).

The article also stated that some 15,000 undernourished students in six Polish university cities were at that time being served one meal a day by the

A.R.A. Additionally, through drafts sold in America against food stored in A.R.A. warehouses in Poland, food donation worth $265,000 had been made for intelligentsia relief, $302,000 for refugee relief, and $90,000 for general relief. The Polish government on its part "contributed to the relief action all the flour, cost of transportation, special purchases of foodstuffs on American credits to a total value of approximately one third of the cost of operation."

Next in importance to food relief was the A.R.A.'s contributions of clothing, either second-hand or manufactured from material shipped from the United States. As pointed out in the same article, through the A.R.A. the children of Poland had received "seven hundred thousand (700,000) clothing outfits, consisting of overcoats, shoes and woolen stockings, and three hundred thousand (300,000) suits of flannelette underclothing."[81]

In 1920 the A.R.A. Polish Mission assisted in procuring 4,600 American freight cars from U.S. Army stocks and in negotiating for 150 new locomotives from the Baldwin Locomotive Works. In 1922, 7,500 additional American freight cars were transferred to Poland on long-term credits from the American government to strengthen the war-torn transportation system. The total deliveries during the thirty-eight months of A.R.A. operations in Poland "amounted to 751,135.6 metric tons valued at the enormous sum of $200,864,857.73." The three basic sums were:[82]

Sold for cash	$ 8,523,937.17
Delivered on credit	163,035,725.16
Benevolence	29,305,195.40
	$200,864,857.73

(For a detailed summary of total relief deliveries to Poland, see Document 22.)

One may only speculate what would have happened without such extensive American assistance. As emphasized by Barber, however:

> It is difficult to estimate the results of those three years of organized relief work in Poland. Perhaps the most important and most far reaching will prove to be the renewed understanding and sympathy between Poland and America flowing from the close contact of Americans and Poles in that trying period of readjustment. Certain it is that to the vision, energy and leadership of Herbert Hoover Poland and America owe in great part the firm establishment in the maelstrom of political and social disorder of post-war Europe of a sister-republic pledged to loyal friendship to the United States in the years to come.[83]

With the visible improvements in the Polish economy, the time had come to wind up the vast American relief commitments. On Hoover's and Director Brown's instructions, Philip S. Baldwin, the last chief of the A.R.A. mission in

Poland, saw Prime Minister Antoni Ponikowski late in February 1922 to inform him that the A.R.A. would phase out on June 1. Baldwin then wrote an official letter outlining projects that the Polish government might undertake after the withdrawal. He suggested the

> feeding of 400,000 children from June 1st to October 1st, 1922; and 300,000 children from October 1st 1922, to June 1st, 1923; *figures reached after careful investigation and conservatively estimating the number of children who will be in dire need of relief after our withdrawal.* . . .

> I need hardly repeat how vitally interested are Mr. Hoover and his Mission in Poland in a prompt and business-like handling of this question of the future. We all keenly realize that the eyes of America are focused upon Poland and the intelligent solution which we shall give to this question. . . .

> It would demonstrate Poland's ability to handle this vital interior problem, and justify that confidence which Mr. Hoover is endeavoring to build up for Poland among the American people and the nations of the world.

While emphasizing what was needed, Baldwin also acknowledged that the Polish Diet, at its general session on February 28, had not only approved the resolution of the Commission on Health and Public Protection to provide the necessary funds to continue child feeding but had also called upon the government "to submit to the Diet at the earliest possible moment a statute conferring on Mr. Hoover the honorary citizenship of Poland for his great humanitarian work in Poland."[84]

At a meeting of its Economic Council on April 3, the government guaranteed assumption of the responsibility for carrying out Baldwin's suggestions. A prominent economist and former prime minister, Władysław Grabski, assumed direction of future P.A.K.P.D. operations. Pleased with the Polish government's reaction, Secretary Hoover sent a congratulatory telegram.

> My colleagues and myself are deeply interested and appreciate the action of the Polish Government in assuming complete responsibility for the feeding of its needy children. The relief that this administration has been able to give to the children of your republic during the past three years has been sent you as a gift from America. . . . Since the inception of our work your Government has given continual increased evidence of your ability and desire to care for your own problems. . . . We beg to confirm to you our withdrawal from Poland on June first next. These many months of cooperative work when American aid has been of assistance to you have, we feel sure, more firmly cemented the bonds of friendship between our two great republics. . . .[85]

In turn, Premier Ponikowski proclaimed the takeover of A.R.A. activities by the P.A.K.P.D. on May 7, 1922, and expressed gratitude for the A.R.A.'s services to Poland. "The entire population of Poland worships the name of Hoover and surrounds with gratitude and esteem all his countrymen who have cooperated with the relief action in Poland. The feeling that the work initiated by Mr. Hoover will not be interrupted, but will be carried on by our nation itself, will be their best reward at the moment of their departure from Poland."[86]

Never before or after this three-year period did Poland and the United States have so intense a relationship based on mutual respect. At no other point were there working in Poland so many dedicated Americans as during that reconstruction period (Documents 23, 24). Never was there such manifold and timely assistance of a similar magnitude given to the Poles by any friendly nation.[87]

Warsaw decided to commemorate the contributions of Hoover and the United States by erecting a monument in a small Hoover Square on the historic Krakowskie Przedmieście thoroughfare. At the entrance to the square two marble stands bore the inscription "Herbert Hoover." The monument, the work of Ksawery Dunikowski, was unveiled at an impressive ceremony on October 29, 1922. As Hugh Gibson described the occasion to Christian Herter:

> We began with a High Mass in the Cathedral said by the Cardinal [Kakowski], and then a stately procession on foot through the slush in company with all the dignitaries of the Country, civil and military, through solid ranks of troops and school children, there being one hundred thousand of the latter backed up along the line of march. It was all extraordinarily well done, and the speeches showed a large appreciation of what the Chief had accomplished in Poland. . . .[88]

Induced no doubt by the example of the A.R.A., the Polish government in 1921 offered to transport American relief materials without charge across its territories to starving Russia. Special trains carried the supplies from Gdańsk to Stołpce, where they were transferred to the wider-gauged Russian cars.[89]

Foreign Minister Konstanty Skirmunt wrote to Baldwin offering humanitarian reasons for assisting Russia despite past difficulties between the two countries.

> The Polish people having known the blessings of relief work on a great scale in time of national sufferings, wishes to do its share in alleviating distress in Russia. . . .
>
> Although Poland has for many years been under the oppression of the Russian yoke, yet the Polish Nation feels that the ill treatment to which they were subjected was caused to a greater extent by the Russian Government,

than by the Russian people. In view of this . . . it is the sincere desire of the Polish Nation to tender a hand of friendship and help to the suffering Russian masses.[90]

Some of Skirmunt's associates believed that he was naive in his amiable gestures to Russia.[91] It seems, however, that due to the A.R.A.'s mediation, the Poles were able to obtain some concessions from the Russians. "The Polish Government asked the A.R.A. to use its good offices in bringing about the ratification of a Polish-Russian general railway agreement, that had been hanging fire for several months. The A.R.A. took up the subject with Moscow, and the agreement was ratified. One clause dealt with and facilitated the return of Polish refugees from Russia."[92]

Poland's cooperation was apparently essential for the implementation of the A.R.A.'s Russian relief operation. On February 17, 1922, Brown cabled Baldwin:

Many thanks for your letter . . . with confirmation of agreement of Poland's efforts to transport 15,000 tons of corn monthly, free of cost to us, for our Russian operation. . . . The problem of transport of the Congressional Appropriation foodstuffs is a difficult one. . . . Some of our ships are ice-bound in the North Sea. . . . While we appreciate the difficulties attending these shipments across Poland, their cooperation has been a great step towards relieving the proposition we are up against.[93]

The unwinding of A.R.A. operations in Poland did not mean that Herbert Hoover lost interest in the country he had helped so effectively. Thanks to his vast international experience, Secretary Hoover rose in stature under Presidents Harding and Coolidge. He was preoccupied with cabinet affairs, but his interest in Europe, and especially in Poland, was never subject to the growing spirit of isolationism during those years. On February 10, 1925, while Hoover was secretary of commerce, Poland obtained "most-favored nation" status. He was also instrumental in sending to Warsaw prominent financial advisers, Edwin Walter Kemmerer of Princeton University—at the end of 1925 and again in 1926—and Charles E. Dewey, former undersecretary of the Treasury—from the end of 1927 until 1930.

PART II

Friend in the White House

When he became a presidential candidate, Hoover naturally was interested in capitalizing on the admiration expressed by Polish Americans, knowing well that as blue-collar workers most of them were registered Democrats. On April 14, 1928, a Republican meeting for various Slavic groups was held at the Cooper Union Auditorium in New York City. Endorsing Hoover's candidacy on behalf of Polish Americans, E. H. Lewiński-Corwin gave an impassioned account of Hoover's A.R.A. contributions to Poland, stressing his "first-hand personal knowledge of international affairs" and his exceptional organizational talents. As secretary of the New York Academy of Medicine, he turned to good account one of Hoover's honors:

> In recognition of his services, the ancient University of Cracow bestowed upon Mr. Hoover an honorary degree of Doctor of Medicine. . . . It was particularly well deserved in this instance, for what degree is more appropriate than the degree of Doctor of Medicine for the man who alleviated more physical suffering, in an efficient, kindly and speedy manner, than any mortal in the history of civilization. . . . Is it not appropriate that the executive guidance of this republic should be placed in the experienced and able hands of the great Dr. Hoover?[94]

The New York daily *Nowy Świat* (New World) editorialized that "Poland and the Poles will never forget the historic work of Mr. Hoover." The *Zgoda* in Chicago proclaimed that "Hoover's record proves that he is a real leader of world-wide experience, his principles are democratic," and the progressive Milwaukee *Kurjer Polski* stated, "As a lover of work, his first thought is for the laboring classes, and the main point of his platform is to secure a living wage." A campaign publication reprinted testimonials of gratitude from the old country and parts of a speech delivered by Paderewski at the Commodore Hotel in New York. Said Paderewski of Hoover:

> Not only did he provide foodstuffs and clothing for needy multitudes, but . . . he enabled my Government to reopen the idle mills of Lodz by giving me spontaneously 27,000 bales of cotton for that purpose.
>
> . . . Hundreds of thousands of our future citizens owe their health and even their lives to him. It was one of the proudest days of my life when, for the first time . . . since Poland's partition, I could open the doors of the ancient council of our kings and receive there with noble songs, this noble son of American democracy.[95]

Paderewski's support was evidently important among Polish-American voters, especially since Hoover's opponent was Al Smith of New York, the first Roman Catholic to seek the presidency. The Republicans must have been well aware of that asset, as indicated by the October 1, 1928 request that Paderewski received from Frederick Walcott, an old associate of Hoover. "The Chairman of our State Republican Committee, J. Henry Roraback, was anxious to have some word from you that might be circulated among the Polish voters of this State in the interests of Mr. Hoover. . . ."[96]

President-Elect Hoover was happy with the support he had obtained from American Polonia. He asked John B. Stetson, the American minister in Warsaw, to transmit to the senders of congratulatory telegrams from Poland his "deep appreciation for their courtesy" and his good wishes. Later Hoover commented on Stetson's evaluation of the Polish attitude toward the election, adding that "the Poles of the United States very generally supported me during the recent election."[97]

Soon after he assumed office Hoover indicated his firm support of both the Polish republic and American Polonia and hailed the loyalty to the United States of Americans of Polish descent. In the message to Benjamin T. Anuszkiewicz of the Polish Legion of the American Army, the president said:

> With you I pay homage to the memory of those American citizens, men and women of Polish extraction who gave their lives for the United States during the World War and who thereby demonstrated the unreserved measure with which they gave their whole loyalty to our common country, forsaking with pure spirits all past allegiance and defending the new even to the death.[98]

In April the president issued a statement for the *Chicago Tribune*'s Paris edition, which was running a special supplement on Poland for the international exhibition in the city of Poznań. He praised Poland's achievements in her first decade of regained independence (Document 25). At the opening of that exhibit on May 16, a temporary bust of Hoover by the sculptor Antoni Janik was unveiled in the American Pavilion by the minister of foreign affairs, August Zaleski. President Hoover agreed to sit for a permanent bust to be erected by the Polish Publishers Association of America. In his letter to A. E. Ruszkiewicz of Buffalo's *Dziennik dla Wszystkich* (Everybody's Daily), Hoover said: "I feel greatly honored . . . and am deeply complimented by your activities in the matter. I will be glad to see Mr. Janik when he arrives, and will try to do my part." He again expressed his attitude toward Poland in answer to the message of Poland's President Ignacy Mościcki on the occasion of General Pułaski's sesquicentennial celebration. Hoover wrote from the White House, "I shall be happy to greet Your Excellency's distinguished delegation and through them assure Your Excellency of my country's gratitude and friendship for Poland."[99]

With the Depression, the president had much less time for Polish problems during the last three years of his troubled administration and had to decline invitations to various festivities. The most important was the fiftieth anniversary of the founding of the largest Polish-American fraternal organization, the Polish National Alliance (Związek Narodowy Polski—Z.N.P.).

Hoover wrote to its president, John Romaszkiewicz, on August 7, 1930, expressing his appreciation for the alliance's constructive contributions (Document 26). A similar message was sent by the president to the Polish Home in Buffalo, New York, on the same occasion. "The Polish people in this country have made a noteworthy contribution to its ideals and development, which deserves the warmest appreciation. The Polish National Alliance has been a most useful agency in furthering community projects in education and human welfare and I wish for it all success in the future."[100]

On August 21 he wrote to John J. Olejniczak, president of the Polish Roman Catholic Union of America, in response to an invitation to attend the tenth anniversary of the "Miracle at the Vistula" in Chicago. Though unable to attend, the president asked, "I will be obliged if you will express my cordial greetings to those present at the celebration and my profound appreciation of the value of the contributions made by the people of Polish extraction to the enriching of our national life."[101]

Besides such routine matters as annual proclamations of Pułaski Memorial Day in October or remarks at the official visits of Polish diplomats, President Hoover was keen to maintain his personal friendship with Paderewski, who was entertained in the White House, as indicated by a telegram of November 16, 1930.

> The President and Mrs. Hoover are delighted that you may be with them even for such a very short visit. Automobiles will meet your train at sixteen on November twenty-fifth. Thinking a quiet rest, probably the most acceptable entertainment for you in the midst of a tour, they are not making any formal occasion during your visit, but simply having a few personal friends in each evening.[102]

According to the account of that two-day visit by Paderewski's secretary, the Polish guests were treated "just like members of the family."[103]

Paderewski donated a statue of the late President Wilson, which was unveiled by President Mościcki in Poznań on July 4, 1931. Unable to attend the ceremony, Hoover sent a message stressing Wilson's friendship for Poland, and it was read by the recently appointed first American ambassador to Poland, John Willys (Document 27).[104]

Official relations between Poland and the United States were strengthened by two acts of Hoover's administration: the U.S. and Polish legations in Warsaw and Washington were raised to ambassador status, and a Treaty of Friendship, Commerce, and Consular Rights was signed. As emphasized by Tytus Filipowicz on March 4, 1930, at the formal presentation of his credentials as the first ambassador of Poland to America, it was Hoover's wish that Poland be represented by a regular ambassador.

I know that it was with great satisfaction that the President of Poland was able to fulfill your desire, because he considered the appointments of an Ambassador of Poland in Washington and of an Ambassador of the United States in Warsaw as the expression of reciprocal sentiments of the Heads of two nations . . . and because this new step tended to strengthen the friendship, increase the volume of trade and add to the feeling of security in Central and Eastern Europe.[105]

In his official reply to Ambassador Filipowicz's remarks, President Hoover expressed his wish that the United States and Poland "maintain with one another the closest and most cordial relations" (Document 28).

The treaty of friendship, prepared by Secretary of State Henry Stimson and Ambassador Filipowicz after three years of negotiations, was ratified by Congress on April 21, 1932, and by Poland a year later.[106] This was the first agreement of that type signed between two countries.

Hoover's secretary of state did not share the concern of his predecessor, Vernon Kellogg, for Polish problems and was sympathetic toward a German revisionist policy. Nevertheless, there is no proof that the president himself ever changed his very friendly disposition toward Poland. With Hoover's increased involvement in problems of the Great Depression, Secretary Stimson acquired substantial independence. Stimson's policies caused great concern in Warsaw that the traditional American friendship was cooling off. Indeed his diary entry for September 20, 1931, clearly indicates that he was considering "a revision of Versailles," in particular a new "treaty with concessions to Germany on the Polish Corridor." To neutralize the rumors that he favored Germany over Poland, Stimson went on record at a press conference that fall that "the question of Polish-German frontiers was a purely European problem in which the American Government had no direct interest."[107] This was to be the official American policy until the Nazi invasion of September 1, 1939.

The alleged support for such threats to the Polish frontier caused great anxiety in Poland. Ambassador Willys reported on October 20, 1931, that it was maintained in Poland that "the United States is so concerned over the security of its financial commitments in Germany that American influence is being aligned on the side of the Reich against Poland."[108] These fears were exacerbated by the actions of the influential chairman of the Senate Foreign Relations Committee, William E. Borah of Idaho. On the eve of the important visit of the French prime minister, Pierre Laval, on October 22, Borah conferred with Hoover. The senator, an old foe of the Versailles Treaty, suggested that France's debts to the United States be cancelled in return for her reducing war reparations from Germany and her cooperation on revision of the "Polish Corridor." Borah then held a press conference with French newsmen and implied that the president was considering frontier revisions in Europe, particularly with regard to the "Polish Corridor." A great deal of importance was attached to Borah's statements, and they stirred up public opinion both at home and abroad.

> Berlin and Budapest were almost beside themselves with joy. Warsaw was enraged, Paris gnashed its teeth. The rank and file in France called Borah a swine; the more cultured damned him deeper with their term "naïve." He raised a bumper crop of cheers and jeers in his own country. . . .

> He said that the Polish Corridor should be returned to Germany and that the former boundaries of Hungary should be restored.[109]

President Hoover was evidently outraged by the anti-Polish suggestion of the "Lion from Idaho." On October 25 the White House issued an unequivocal communiqué: "A press statement that the President has proposed any revision of the Polish Corridor is absolutely without foundation. The President has made no suggestions of any such character."[110]

Aware of the growing danger of Hitlerism, Poland's strongman, Marshal Pułsudski, feared that another world war might start in exactly that area and toyed with the idea of a preventive war against Germany before she became too strong. With the uncertainties in Washington, he instructed Ambassador Filipowicz to bring Poland's position directly to President Hoover's personal attention:

> Poland would not consider any settlement of the Polish corridor other than the maintenance of the *status quo*. Poland would absolutely refuse to enter into any discussion whatsoever of that subject with any neutral nation. Poland believes that there is at almost any moment the danger of the invasion of Polish territory by German irregular troops. If this should occur the whole Polish army would be immediately mobilized and march into Germany to settle the thing once and for all, and they would not be influenced by any action of the League of Nations or anyone else.[111]

John C. Wiley, the chargé d'affaires in Poland, claimed in a dispatch of December 2, 1931, that Piłsudski's warning was primarily designed to silence American supporters of German revisionism. "The Marshal . . . may have thought that by alarming the American government with the danger of war, it would, out of anxiety for the security of things in Germany, take effective steps to put an end to Corridor discussions in the United States." At the same time Wiley admitted that Piłsudski's message might be more than a bluff, that his threat of a Polish preventive attack on Germany was "probably not an empty one."[112]

The Polish-German frontier problem, aggravated by Nazi agitation, again came to the fore in Washington in 1932. In May and June Polish demarches focused on the high-handed German policy toward Gdańsk.[113]

The Japanese-Chinese crisis in East Asia precipitated American efforts toward reduction and limitation of armaments, and the Polish government approved them. At the Geneva Conference in the summer of 1932, nineteen delegations spoke on President Hoover's plan of disarmament. Hugh Gibson represented the United States at the conference. In his July 8 trans-Atlantic telephone conversation with Undersecretary of State William R. Castle, he said that despite the fact that Polish and some other delegations did not speak, they "made it clear that they are enthusiastic in their support" of the Hoover plan.[114]

The last foreign policy issue of Hoover's administration was his moratorium on war debts, including German reparation payments. He considered such a moratorium necessary to stop the worldwide depression. Only Finland was able to pay her debt to America. Poland defaulted in 1932 after six months of protracted negotiations. Although Hoover was in principle against the outright cancellation of the debts, he conceded to one-year postponements for a number of countries in real financial trouble. On November 22, "owing to the general financial and economic situation of the world," Ambassador Filipowicz asked for a two-year postponement of Poland's $3,302,980 payment (a large part of it being the semiannual interest on the unpaid principal) due on December 15. He made it clear that the Polish government "would welcome the opportunity of a conference with the Government of the United States in order to discuss the conditions" of such a postponement.

Acting Secretary of State Castle, who was much closer to Hoover than Secretary Stimson, answered on November 26 that any review of existing intergovernmental financial obligations was constitutionally reserved for the Congress, which lately had acted through the agency of the War Debt Commission in similar situations. He continued:

> I am not oblivious to the fact that the world depression and the concurrent fall of prices has increased the weight of debts in many parts of the world; nor to the fact that the decrease in international trade has increased the difficulties of obtaining foreign exchange. . . . On the other hand, it must also be remembered that these incidents of the depression have also fallen with great weight upon the American people and the effects upon them directly as taxpayers or otherwise of any modification of an agreement with respect to debts due this country cannot be disregarded. . . .

The attitude of the President, therefore, is that . . . no authority lies with
the Executive to grant such an extension, and no facts have been placed in
our possession which could be presented to the Congress for favorable
consideration.

In response, Filipowicz submitted a lengthy note to the State Department on
December 8 with statistics supporting the Polish application. Among other
arguments, it was stated that the rate of interest in the original 1924 agreement was "too burdensome" and that, being a predominantly agricultural
country, Poland had been particularly affected by the decline of the prices
of farm products in the world market. As to commercial relations, Warsaw
claimed that Poland bought ten times as much from the United States as
she sold there.

The well-documented request of the Polish government was cold-
shouldered by Stimson, who replied officially on December 15:

> The President of the United States is prepared, through whatever agency
> may seem appropriate, to cooperate with the Polish Government in surveying
> the entire situation and in considering what means may be taken to bring
> about the restoration of stable currencies and exchange, the revival of trade,
> and the recovery process.
>
> I believe that there are important avenues of mutual advantage which should
> be thoroughly explored. Such an examination does not imply cancellation.
>
> My Government, however, has not been able to reach the conclusion that
> a postponement of the December 15th payment from the Polish Government
> to the United States is necessary because of its effect on the problem of
> recovery.[115]

Hoover tried, without much success, to get the new president-elect involved
in bipartisan action on his idea of a moratorium on war debts and war reparations. With Roosevelt's aloofness in that delicate matter, nothing was
achieved, and the World War I debts remained unpaid as of 1933.[116]

The last official acts of the lame-duck president with regard to Poland
involved a formal reception for outgoing Ambassador Filipowicz on January 3, 1933, and the presentation of credentials on January 17 to Poland's
second ambassador to the United States, Stanisław Patek. Avoiding the
debt payment issue, President Hoover reassured the veteran diplomat:

> I greatly appreciate the sentiments of good will towards the American people
> which you have expressed on behalf of the Polish nation and I need not
> assure you that we have followed with friendly sympathy the progress that

your country has made in the years that have elapsed since the reestablishment of an independent Poland. The good will of the Polish people is highly
valued by the people of the United States. . . .[117]

The election of 1932, disastrous for Hoover and his Grand Old Party,
may have made him somewhat bitter toward Polish-American voters who,
sensitive to the promises of the New Deal, overwhelmingly returned to the
Democratic fold. As late as October 31 Hoover had still been hopeful that
"the American citizens of Polish extraction" had "remained firm in their
support" of him and the Republican party.[118]

Regardless of the Polish-American vote, the president still appreciated
Polonia's deep attachment to American institutions. In December he praised
their contribution to Washington's Bicentennial.

> It is in keeping with their splendid record of loyalty to the institutions of the
> United States that the American citizens of Polish origin have so fully partici-
> pated in the nationwide observance of the George Washington Bicentennial.
> It is doubly appropriate that they should do so because of the noble services
> rendered to the cause of American liberty by General Pulaski and other
> Polish lovers of freedom. I am deeply appreciative of the work of the Polish
> American George Washington Bicentennial Committee and their fellow
> compatriots.[119]

The only possible indication of any annoyance on Hoover's part is the
relative paucity of correspondence on Polish matters or public commitments
to Polish causes for almost five years. Yet an obvious explanation for that
long gap between 1933 and 1938 is that Hoover was preoccupied and frustrated with his own nation's blaming him for the Depression.

PART III

Friend in Opposition

Early in 1938 Hoover decided to spend three months in Europe to personally investigate "the cause or causes of the economic collapse of Europe in
1931."[120] One of the countries visited on that tour was Poland. On the way to
Finland from Berlin, where at the U.S. ambassador's request he accepted the
invitations of Göring and Hitler, he stopped first in Poznań on March 11
and then visited Kraków. Everywhere he was enthusiastically received by
thousands of young people, many of them former beneficiaries of the A.R.A.
In Kraków he went to the crypt of St. Leonard at the Wawel Castle to pay

homage to the remains of Marshal Piłsudski, who had died in May 1935. He also left a wreath of roses at Kościuszko's tomb in the Wawel Cathedral.[121] Hoover briefly stopped in Warsaw, where he visited, among others, the American director of the YMCA, Paul Super, and his wife, Margaret. His old Polish friends were no longer there—Ignacy Paderewski and Wincenty Witos lived in self-exile. Piłsudski's undemocratic successors were not comparable in stature to the previous charismatic leaders.

When the war broke out, Hoover decided once again to offer his services for Polish relief. He was officially approached by Ambassador Jerzy Potocki on September 16, 1939, and the new Commission for Relief in Poland was organized on September 25 with many old A.R.A. personnel as officers. Herbert Hoover was honorary chairman; Chauncey McCormick, chairman; and Maurice Pate. president. The directors were Hugh Gibson, W. Hallam Tuck, Edgar Rickard, Perrin C. Galpin, Lewis L. Strauss, Theodore Abel, Frederick C. Walcott, and Mrs. Vernon Kellogg. Hoover undertook the responsibility for negotiating with the governments concerned and for securing financial support by issuing statements and making public speeches. His first address, "The Spirit of Poland," was delivered on Pulaski Memorial Day, October 11, 1939. Citing history and his first-hand experience, he expressed firm belief in the unconquerable spirit of the Polish people under duress (Document 29).

While Hoover's assistants attended to the major problems of the purchase of relief supplies and transportation in the United States, William C. McDonald, who had been stationed in Warsaw during September 1939 to help in the evacuation of American citizens, was asked to conduct from Switzerland negotiations with the Germans for the distribution of food and medical supplies. In Hoover's words, the relief activities at the outset were mainly efforts concentrated upon two programs: "The supply of food and clothing to the underfed children in the congested districts and ghettos in Poland, and the care of Polish refugees, now scattered over Europe." To achieve these ends, "Mr. Pate set up canteens, under the care of Polish women, which provided special meals to 200,000 undernourished children and aged persons daily in Poland."[122] The route of the shipments of food and clothing was from neutral America to neutral Sweden and then across the Baltic Sea to Hamburg or Gdańsk.

General Władysław Sikorski, prime minister of the Polish government in exile, thanked Hoover on December 6, 1939, for his new efforts and asked him to persist in this noble work. His government (residing in Angers, France) set up a refugee relief fund and made an initial donation of $186,225 on February 15, 1940.

To finance growing relief needs, the Hoover commission supported various appeals of Polish-American organizations in the United States. At a mass meeting held in Chicago, the largest center of American Polonia, Hoover delivered a fiery appeal on February 10 (Document 30). During the first months of its activities the commission received approximately $400,000, but the scattered charitable efforts and the irregular donations of the Polish government in exile were insufficient for major assistance. Therefore, for the first time since his tenure as secretary of commerce, the former president decided to appeal in person to a key congressional committee. On February 29 he obtained a special hearing before the House Foreign Affairs Committee, chaired by Rep. Sol Bloom (Document 31). Hoover advocated a $50 million appropriation to the American Red Cross to undertake food and medical relief for some seven million Polish citizens "badly in need of outside help."[123] When Congress approved the appropriation, the Red Cross undertook medical aid to Poland, but Hoover's organization received none of the funds for food relief.

Hoover became more involved in Polish affairs in the early months of 1940 than he had been since 1919. Perhaps it was psychological compensation for his talents being ignored by the FDR administration. To stimulate charitable contributions, his commission organized a rally at New York City's Madison Square Garden on March 12 with the former president as the main speaker (Document 32). Expressing his continuing faith in the future of the Polish nation as a free and democratic country, he assured his vast audience: "There will be no permanent peace and therefore no stability in the world as long as oppression of a great and independent race continues in Poland."[124]

Again on April 28 Hoover and General Józef Haller, a senior cabinet member without portfolio of the Polish government, addressed another public meeting in New York City. Urging the immediate alleviation of Polish suffering, Hoover expressed his undiminished hope in Poland's resurrection. "The soul of a people is forged from its tradition, instincts, arts, language, literature, music, heroic struggles and its heroic men and women. It may be oppressed, its houses and cities may be destroyed, its people exiled and enslaved, but the spirit of a great people cannot be crushed. . . ." Hoover blamed Soviet Russia for taking supplies from the agricultural areas of incorporated eastern Poland and warned that the task of delivery by sea had been rendered impossible by the war on Norway and, with the occupation of Denmark, the closing of the Baltic to all shipping. In view of these new complications he anticipated that American supplies would have to "make long railway journeys from the Mediterranean to save the lives of the people of Poland." He envisaged great sums of relief money needed—"upwards of

$30,000,000"—and expressed at the same time the hope that "Congress will appropriate some of the surplus food stuffs which will rot in America and send them to the starving people."[125]

Hoover's old friend Paderewski, elected chairman of the Polish Council of National Unity, came to the United States in November 1940 to help Poland. He again became associated with Hoover, especially through the Paderewski Fund for Polish Relief, headquartered in New York.[126] Pleased that Col. William J. Donovan agreed to serve as president of the Paderewski Fund, Hoover had written to him on March 17, 1940; "There is no cause more worthy of the effort of yourself and your colleagues than providing funds for the saving of life in Poland. I know of no one who can give more effective leadership than yourself."[127] (When Paderewski died on June 29, 1941, Hoover wrote a moving message, which was conveyed by Maurice Pate to Paderewski's friends [Document 33]). Until his last years Hoover was in correspondence with the Paderewski Foundation's officers, particularly its chairman, Edward S. Witkowski.[128]

On the basis of past experience, Hoover realized that private charity would be insufficient. Frustrated with the slow pace of fund raising, Hoover told Norman Davis, president of the American Red Cross:

> I won't go on unless I have five million dollars immediately from the Polish Government. . . . I have to have that for a working capital fund. The need is urgent. I would like to start shiploads going in that direction at once. We could get them under way in a week if they would put up the money. It is useless to try to finance five million dollars with any public giving. The whole thing should be donations from governments.[129]

Sikorski's government quickly reacted. On May 11, 1940, at a special cabinet session, Herbert Hoover was officially asked to accept responsibility for relief of the population of occupied Poland. Minister of Foreign Affairs Zaleski asked Hoover by cable "to start operations immediately." He proposed that the Polish government "negotiate with British and French Governments terms of blockade clearance for food supplies for famished urban and rural populations in Poland on principle of continuity of relief action" and specified that such relief should first cover milk, fats, and clothing. The government declared its readiness to place $1 million at Hoover's disposal immediately and another "million dollars in sterling and French francs for relief purchases in pound and franc monetary areas." In addition the Polish government pledged a sum of gold that had been deposited with the Bank of Romania in Bucharest after the Polish campaign in the fall of 1939. Anticipating complications with Bucharest, Zaleski suggested placing "at

President Hoover's disposal requisite means of payment for relief purchases on markets designated by Allies and in consultation with Allies' purchasing organizations up to amount of Rumanian gold deposit not otherwise utilised."[130]

On June 6, 1940, the Polish government gave another $400,200. By summer the total donations for Hoover's commission amounted to about $6 million including the Polish gold worth $3 million, deposited in Romania. (When the United States entered the war in December 1941, unsuccessful attempts by a representative of Hoover's commission to retrieve the gold from Bucharest were suspended.) The Polish government, evacuated to London after the debacle of France, sent another $100,000 on January 21, 1941.

Hoover's negotiations for delivery of supplies were originally conducted through the German embassy in Washington. The officials were considered by Hoover to be "most co-operative," and they issued certificates of immunity from U-boat attacks provided "neutral vessels were used." It was a different story with the British blockade against the delivery of any food to German-occupied territory. As long as Chamberlain was in office, Hoover managed to obtain permits for relief shipments. When Churchill became prime minister in May 1940, however, "he soon stopped all permits for food relief to Poland." As told by a disappointed Hoover: "It was only by the incredible tenacity of Maurice Pate and our men in Europe that a meager stream of food and medical relief continued to trickle to Poland for nearly two more years. Beyond doubt, this saved thousands of lives."[131]

A pathetic appeal from Polish relief workers was sent on April 2, 1941. It gave an appalling picture of the food situation and closed with bitter words: "Under such tragic conditions of existence we cannot understand the lack of aid from outside. Is it possible that men of such calibre as Mr. Hoover cannot find the means of saving us from death through starvation?"[132]

Despite Pate's valiant efforts to help Poland, the political attitudes of the belligerent powers prevented substantial American assistance (unlike with Belgium a quarter of a century earlier). Hoover was greatly disappointed. Moreover, his relationship with President Roosevelt was entirely different from his association with Woodrow Wilson.

Nevertheless, what was achieved during those first years of the war was of immense value, as shown by the numerous expressions of gratitude preserved by Hoover. On September 15, 1940, a message came directly from the Central Polish Relief Organization (Rada Główna Opiekuńcza—R.G.O.). Its chairman, Count Adam Ronikier, assured Hoover that American gifts were given only to those for whom they were intended and pleaded for continued aid. He again cabled Hoover on November 1 to ask for assistance to help the population to survive the coming winter. The primate of Poland, August Cardinal Hlond, wrote from his seclusion in unoccupied France on March 15, 1941: "As the head of the Church in Poland, I express to you my gratitude and recognition for the help given already to my compatriots both in the persecuted country and on this sorrowful emigration. Especially I send the expression of my gratitude to Mr. Hoover. . . ."[133]

With the German occupation of western Europe, the exiled governments of Norway, Belgium, and Holland and de Gaulle's Government of Free France appealed for relief organizations for their occupied lands. The Committee on Food for the Small Democracies was organized on November 18, 1940, with some 800 Americans as cosponsors and Hoover as its honorary chairman.

The British government again raised objections to large systematic imports through their naval blockade of Nazi-occupied Europe. Consequently, as in World War I, Hoover proposed in January 1941 to undertake a trial relief operation in Belgium, "which if successful, could be applied to Poland." In his letter to the Polish ambassador in Washington, Jan Ciechanowski, on April 23, 1941, Hoover complained that statements on the part of several exiled personalities indicated that under British pressure they too were opposed to his new relief operations. He even raised the "question of good faith by Polish officials."[134] Ciechanowski denied that the Polish government had ever "opposed any practical scheme for relief of the lamentable situation of the populations of the countries invaded and oppressed by Germany or Soviet Russia." With regard to the British blockade, he told Hoover:

> The Polish Government represents a fighting Poland, actively engaged in this war alongside of her British Ally. They regard the blockade as one of the most effective means to ultimate victory, and they have ample evidence that this view is fully supported by the united opinion of all representative patriotic organizations in Poland. . . . I must reject the allegation that the Polish Government are acting under any outside pressure in the matter of Polish Relief. . . . The Polish Government are entirely independent in their policies and are fully aware of their responsibilities in regard to their duties as the Government of a nation determined to fight for its Independence, —whatever the cost.[135]

The final result of the controversy, as Pate explained, was that "in the growing bitterness of the war and more extensive blockade measures, Mr. Hoover's organizations were prohibited from shipment of any but minor supplies, and eventually all effort, including Poland and Finland, was stopped by the combatant governments."[136]

As official leader of the opposition in the United States, Hoover often expressed his critical views of American foreign policy, speaking out against entanglement in European conflicts. Already in a 1938 speech delivered after his tour of Europe, he advocated keeping America out of the coming trouble. "I found most nations in Europe convinced that we would be inevitably drawn into the next great war as in the last. Some people build confident hope upon it. But every phase of this picture should harden our resolves that we keep out of other people's wars. Nations in Europe need to be convinced that this is our policy. . . ."[137] After the outbreak of hostilities in Europe (though he was concerned about the Poles), he maintained the same posture, as expressed even in the title of an article in the *Saturday Evening Post:* "We Must Keep Out." He voiced his conviction that "the American people will be confronted with the issue of war and peace as long as this war in Europe lasts," but at the same time he advocated that America keep out of such wars. "We are incensed at the dictatorships, their ideologies, and their aggressions. We sympathize with Great Britain, France and Poland. Our danger is that our indignation will displace our reason."[138]

Ever since his initial opposition to the recognition of Communist Russia, Hoover had been consistently anti-Soviet and was particularly annoyed with Stalin's duplicity in the case of Poland, Finland, and the Baltic States. In an article, "Russian Misadventure," originally published in the April 27, 1940 issue of *Colliers,* Hoover directly attacked President Roosevelt's policy toward the USSR and the cupidity of American businessmen in their indiscriminate sales to the Communist agressor country (Document 34). In an article for *Liberty Magazine* Hoover named the nine Horsemen of the Apocalypse, adding to War, Death, Famine, and Pestilence five new destroyers of mankind: "Imperialism, the destroyer of the Independence of nations; Intolerance, the destroyer of the minorities; State-ism, the destroyer of personal liberty; Atheism, the destroyer of faith; and Hate, the destroyer of the unity of mankind. . . . Imperialism has already trampled down the Independence of Ethiopia, Czechoslovakia, Poland, Albania, and Denmark. We have witnessed attacks upon China, Finland, and Norway, unable to defend themselves, and the invasion of Holland and Belgium." As a result of the war, he observed, "many of the smaller nations are already on rations. And in invaded countries there is already famine. It sweeps over Poland."[139]

In spite of his firm stand against armed intervention in the European war, Hoover was neither a defeatist nor a pacifist. To help in dispelling the hysteria that resulted from Hitler's sudden invasion of western European democracies, he said in a radio address on May 27, 1940: "Our people are justly alarmed for our own safety, and some of them are more panicky than the people in Paris and London. There is no occasion for panic. There is need for speed"—speed in defense measures in case of a possible invasion of the Western Hemisphere.[140]

Prevented from participating in any aspect of the American war effort, Hoover kept in touch with his Polish friends and read their literature such as Ignacy Matuszewski's anti-Soviet pamphlet, *What Poland Wants.* Like most of them, he was increasingly critical of the concessions of Roosevelt and Churchill to Stalin at the expense of Poland. He was also kept abreast of events in occupied Poland by Maurice Pate, who continued to do whatever he could for Polish children and prisoners of war.

A characteristic story about Hoover was told in a release of the Polish Telegraph Agency on April 27, 1944, about a girl in an army uniform watching a performance of "The Merry Widow" in New York.

> As she listened to Jan Kiepura, the Polish star of the operetta, sing the popular Polish folk song, "Kujawiak," which Kiepura has made a part of the show, she began to sob. . . .
>
> The portly, modest-looking man sitting in the next seat observed this.
>
> "Don't be discouraged," he said, "I expect Poland to be free again."
>
> The girl thanked him and ceased her sobbing.
>
> When they left the theatre he shook her hand. "Keep your chin up," he said.
>
> "Would you please tell me your name?" she inquired. "I would like to remember it."
>
> "Oh," he said, "it's Hoover—Herbert Hoover." He tipped his hat and walked away. . . .[141]

In October 1944 Hoover was visited by Ambassador Ciechanowski. According to the latter's report, "Hoover expressed a belief that at Teheran President Roosevelt undertook an obligation towards Stalin to preserve a passive policy towards the Polish question and that he had agreed to the Curzon Line with compensation for Poland in the West." Hoover was convinced that at Teheran "Poland was double-crossed," not only by Stalin, but also, unfortunately, by Roosevelt. In answer to the ambassador's obvious question—What should Poland do?—the former president optimistically replied: "If it came out into the open that Russia is striving to control Poland . . . then you will get such indignation and protest from American public opinion between the Atlantic and Pacific Oceans that no American Government could conduct an appeasing policy toward the Soviet Union." When Ciechanowski observed that the Polish government could not interfere in internal American politics as long as direct negotiations might bring positive results, Hoover promised that "when the need arose he personally would undertake to launch an appeal to American public opinion in order to enlist its support for Poland."[142]

Disapproving of Roosevelt's policies, Hoover looked forward to a Republican victory in 1944, even though he did not see eye to eye with Thomas

Dewey either. He endorsed Pate's refusal to accept Herbert Lehman's offer to look after Polish interests in the newly created United Nations Relief and Rehabilitation Administration. Pate wrote to "the Chief" on August 9, 1944: "I would be very glad to do my bit for Poland in her present predicament, but the whole approach to relief under the present setup is so confused that I feel I would not be in a position to render a real service. Therefore I'm sticking to my prisoners of war work to the very end. . . ."[143]

Originally less critical of the Yalta decisions than of those reached in Teheran, Hoover gradually learned that as far as Poland was concerned, it was simply another implementation of the assumption that the big powers have the right to decide the fate of the smaller states, even their Allies, without consulting their representatives.[144] Perhaps he hoped at the beginning that the free and unfettered election formula would be implemented in the Soviet-occupied territories. By March 1945, however, Hoover voiced his disapproval of the Yalta decisions on East-Central Europe. Criticizing the former Dumbarton Oaks proposals with regard to the revision of wartime treaties, he suggested that at the forthcoming United Nations conference in San Francisco "a provision for the revision of onerous or inapplicable treaties or the wrongs of imposed settlements" be submitted by the American delegation.

> The future of nations cannot be frozen. . . . America for all time will sorrow for the fate of Finland, of Estonia, of Latvia, of Lithuania, the partition of Poland, and other states that will be partly or wholly submerged by this war. We cannot even think of another war to secure their freedoms, but we do not need to sacrifice our ideals by acquiescing in their plight. . . .[145]

In July 1945 the United States withdrew its recognition of the exiled Arciszewski government in London in order to establish diplomatic relations with the Communist-controlled provisional government of Edward Osóbka-Morawski in Poland. Hoover did not hide his anger in a letter to Michael Kwapiszewski, a ranking Polish diplomat in Washington. "You know that I consider the whole Polish settlement an outrage on American ideals and purposes in this war. When statesmen run counter to certain fundamentals they create a cancer that will not be healed except by surgical action."[146]

In connection with the Potsdam Conference of July, Hoover authorized Christopher T. Emmet to add his name to those who appealed to the U.S. delegation on behalf of Poland. The signatories voiced strong reservations about U.S. acquiescence to the Polish settlement and demanded "the supervision of the Polish elections not to be left just in the hands of a government overwhelmingly manned by hold-overs from the Lublin regime." Hoover wrote from California: "I am sorry the memorial caught up with me too late for signature. I am all for it, and you may include my name if it is not too late."[147]

With Truman's succession to the White House, Hoover was asked by the new chief executive for advice in relief matters in liberated Europe. With the end of hostilities, the world was again confronted with a great famine, which reached threatening proportions by February 1946. In cooperation with Secretary of Agriculture Clinton P. Anderson, a preliminary survey was made. It showed that the United States, Canada, Australia, and Argentina were the only countries with a surplus of food, whereas forty-three nations with a total population of about 1.8 billion "were very seriously deficient in food supplies," and that mass starvation might hit over 800 million people. Hoover recommended relief operations striving "for a goal through overseas supplies of at least 1,500 calories per diem per person and if possible, 1,800."[148]

To coordinate relief efforts, the Truman administration decided to send Hoover, Hugh Gibson, Maurice Pate, and D. A. Fitzgerald, the eminent agricultural analyst, on a fact-finding mission to twenty-five countries. They left the United States in the latter part of March 1946 and returned early in May. This was the last time Hoover visited Poland, and it was not an easy visit for the seventy-two-year-old man. Throughout his public life he abhorred Communism, and he disapproved of the Communist take-over of Poland. As an official representative on a special relief mission, however, he had to restrain his political comments.

Upon his arrival in Warsaw on March 28, he paid a visit to the party boss, Bolesław Bierut. As told by the U.S. ambassador in Poland, Arthur Bliss Lane, during this courtesy visit Hoover outlined the scope of his mission. He offered its services to assist the Poles in solving the acute food problem, which was expected to reach "the critical stage of starvation by the first week of May, unless sufficient grain supplies were imported in the meantime." On the twenty-ninth Hoover met with Prime Minister Osóbka-Morawski, the two vice-premiers, Władysław Gomułka (Communist) and Stanisław Mikołajczyk (Peasant party), and a group of Polish experts "to devise means by which the tragedy of famine could be averted." His recommendation for the adoption of food rationing was questioned by the Polish officials "on the ground that the people had been so accustomed under the Nazi occupation to disobey regulations they would not observe any food restrictions which the government might now impose."[149]

Hoover had asked Ambassador Lane that he keep social engagements to a minimum and that "no lavish entertainment be given to his party." But the new rulers of Poland gave a sumptuous dinner in his honor at the historic Belweder Palace. It consisted of "ten courses of elaborate dishes" and must have seemed particularly incongruous to Hoover, recalling "the impassioned speeches of government ministers that very morning, stressing the danger of famine."[150]

In his remarks at that dinner, Hoover made the point: "There may be differences in the thinking of the American people from that of the Polish Government on some subjects, but no matter how important these problems may be, the purpose of my Mission is solely the problem of food. . . . In this America has but one object and that is to save human life." He also felt it important to emphasize the ties between America and Poland: "Today, one-fifth of the Polish race live within the United States. And a stronger bond even than this is the sympathy of the American people for suffering, and their admiration for the gallantry of the Polish people." Obviously referring to their new predicament, he remarked, "If history teaches anything, it is that from the unquenchable vitality of the Polish race, Poland will rise again from her ashes."[151] Two days later Hoover delivered a more technical speech in Warsaw (Document 35).

Ambassador Lane recalled an unpleasant incident with security officials during the visit. The ambassador had invited the former president, Hugh Gibson, Maurice Pate, an American interpreter—Lt. William Tonesk— Premier Osóbka-Morawski, and Vice-Premiers Gomułka and Mikołajczyk for an informal dinner. The ambassador was approached by Poland's chief of protocol with the prime minister's request to bring his own interpreter, to which Lane replied that he would prefer not to increase the number of those invited to a small, intimate party and that Mikołajczyk, Pate, and Tonesk were familiar with both English and Polish. Later the same day he received an ultimatum: unless his interpreter were invited, the prime minister would be unable to come. Lane inferred from this that "it was obvious that the government desired to have on hand an independent interpreter to listen to any conversation of a political nature which Mikołajczyk might have with Hoover. . . ."[152]

Even though there were no public demonstrations arranged for Hoover, Ambassador Lane recounts: "When he entered or left the hospitals or schools . . . he was cheered spontaneously and wholeheartedly. The sincerity of the cheering was similar to that which had greeted Eisenhower; markedly different from the regimented demonstrations in honor of the Soviet marshals and of Marshal Tito."[153]

Soon after his return to New York, Hoover had to defend the ambassador in a letter to Secretary of State James F. Byrnes.

This morning press quotes President Bierut of Poland criticizing Ambassador Lane and implying different attitudes of General Eisenhower and myself

in some manner detrimental to the Ambassador. . . . I wish to assure you
that in Ambassador Lane you have a courageous skilled representative who
has a most difficult role in dealing with a puppet government whose existence
and policies are a daily violation of the letter and especially the spirit of the
Atlantic Charter and the Yalta Agreement.[154]

Realizing that the postwar Polish regime was just a "puppet government,"
Hoover was delighted to learn that Stanisław Mikołajczyk (the non-
Communist Peasant party leader who, under pressure from Churchill and
Roosevelt, agreed to serve in the provisional government as vice-premier
and minister of agriculture) had managed to escape after the faked election
of 1947. Hoover and Gibson sent a joint cable to London: "For Mikołajczyk
all good wishes delighted news your safe arrival." When he received an
autographed copy of Mikołajczyk's book, *The Rape of Poland,* in 1949
Hoover wrote to the author, "I shall read every word of it just as soon as I
am done with my present appointment."[155]

In August 1947 Hoover recommended further "charitable efforts on
behalf of the children and destitutes" as they were "both worthy and needy."
He understood that this was "not only in the interest of those in Poland but
also in the interest of the United States and the world." He believed that
it was important "not to cease such charitable efforts to those who are in
need because of those who now dominate the Polish people."[156]

Aware of the importance of historical documentation, Hoover showed a
special interest in the growth of the archival collections of the Hoover Library
on War at Stanford. He evidently was proud of the stacks filled with Polish
materials. He praised David Dallin for the book *Forced Labor in Soviet
Russia*—"one of the most important contributions to world understanding of
what this situation is." Although the evidence given in that book by Dallin
and Boris Nicolaevsky impressed him as convincing, Hoover wrote on
September 2, 1947:

I am wondering whether a little further research into the Polish documentation might not be of importance. The War Library at Stanford University
has been negotiating for the material from Anders' Army and I am told that
among this material, there are about 15 thousand identification cards from
Polish soldiers who were formerly in Siberia work camps, together with a
statement from each one of them. If we should secure the material, I would
be glad to interest myself in putting it at your disposal—if you wish.[157]

To the end of his life Hoover continued to speak out about the plight of
the Poles. In a letter to Leon T. Walkowicz to be used on September 1, 1949,
in connection with the tenth anniversary of the outbreak of World War II
he stated:

This is not an occasion for celebration. It is a day for mourning. We should express our horror at the attack upon Poland and our grief that allied policies sold the freedom of Poland to the Communists. We can be assured that the spirit of independence for Poland and free men and women in Poland still lives as in the past, and free Poland will rise again.[158]

In a written statement for the *Polish Review* Hoover wrote about the betrayal of Poland by the Western Allies (Document 36). Hoover had more and more misgivings about Stalin's policy toward East-Central Europe. In 1950 he openly came out for expelling the Soviet Union and its satellites from the United Nations. In this Lane supported Hoover.[159] Hoover's speech before the Republican National Convention in July 1952 criticized the Yalta commitments, and in 1954 he condemned the Democratic presidents for the appeasement and surrender involved in signing the Teheran, Yalta, and Potsdam treaties with Stalin's Russia.[160] Speaking at his eightieth birthday celebration in West Branch, Iowa, Hoover used the fate of East-Central Europe as a warning against further encroachments of the executive power upon the legislative in the field of foreign affairs. He attacked such executive agreements as the American recognition of Soviet Russia in 1933 and the "tacit alliance with Soviet Russia," which helped in spreading "Communism over the earth." He singled out acquiescence in the annexation by Russia of the Baltic states . . . and the partition of Poland at Teheran," which, he claimed, "extinguished the liberties of tens of millions of people. Worse still was the appeasement and surrender at Yalta of ten nations to slavery."[161]

In his numerous communications with Polish-American organizations, Hoover stressed the need for their active involvement in all possible efforts to help the people of Poland. In a message to the Polish Falcons of America, Hoover wrote in 1957: "The people of Polish descent have made great contributions to the development of our country. They have taken a proper interest in the fate of their fatherland, and if Poland is to be redeemed from its present slavery that redemption will be greatly contributed to by the steadfastness of the people of Polish descent in the United States."[162]

Hoover believed that political exiles also have an important function to perform for their respective motherlands. In a message sent to the International Peasant Union at its congress in Paris in October 1956, he told its president, Stanisław Mikołajczyk: "Sometimes this wholly wicked and unnatural domination of peoples whose inner hopes are for freedom must fail. But the time of its failure and the salvation of their countrymen may be advanced by years by the sympathetic action of those in exile. I wish you every success."[163]

It was, however, the captive peoples themselves about whom Hoover was greatly concerned in his last years. When approached in April 1953 by

Frederick R. Dolbeare, vice-president of the National Committee for A Free Europe, to prepare a radio message for Polish National Day on May 3, he reaffirmed his faith in the Polish nation (Document 37). When asked for a Christmas message for Radio Free Europe by its director, W. J. Conver Egan, Hoover wrote:

> History has constantly demonstrated that virile races cannot long be held in bondage by other nations. The attempt to hold the virile peoples of Czecho-slovakia, Poland, Rumania, Hungary, and Bulgaria under Russian domina-tion has all the certainties of a crash that already has met colonialism in other parts of the world. Hope and faith of freedom never die in great races.[164]

In his speech to the Inter-American Bar Association delivered in Dallas on April 16, 1956, Hoover deplored the fact that "the peoples of Estonia, Latvia, Lithuania, Poland, Roumania, Hungary, Yugoslavia and Czecho-slovakia have descended from free men into the abyss of Communism"[165] Maurice Pate, as executive director of the United Nations International Children's Emergency Fund, passed to "the Chief" the encouraging news of the 1956 anti-Stalinist upheaval in Poland which brought Gomułka to power.[166] Despite some hopeful improvements, Hoover realized that Poland remained a captive country controlled from Moscow. For that tragic state of affairs, he mainly blamed the political phenomena of ruthless power politics, which, in a radio broadcast on April 5, 1959, he termed "This Crisis in the Principles and Morals in International Relations."

> For a recent example, I need only point to the agreements at Yalta and Pots-dam, which provided for free elections in Poland, Czechoslovakia, Hungary, Yugoslavia, and Rumania to establish their own forms of free governments. Those elections were prevented, or they were never free.
>
> The bitter lesson from this experience was that the Western World failed to stand firm and united in holding to those agreements. And so we stood by and witnessed the death of freedom in five nations.[167]

Herbert Hoover could be compassionate not only toward suffering children but also toward oppressed and forgotten nationalities. Perhaps the documentation presented in this study of the "Polish Chapter" in his public life will somewhat help to dispel the stereotyped and unfair image of America's thirty-first president as an aloof, almost inhuman, figure. Until the end of his life, Hoover openly opposed the big powers' high-handed policy and remained faithful to the Wilsonian doctrine of self-determination. With his death in 1964 the captive peoples of East-Central Europe lost one of their staunchest friends.

Photographs

Polish American "Gray Samaritans" of YWCA arriving in Warsaw, Summer 1919. (*HIA*)

Polish children fed by American Relief Administration. (*Hoover Presidential Library [HPL] West Branch, Iowa*)

Monument commemorating Hoover's aid, erected in Warsaw's Hoover Square on the Krakowskie Przedmieście thoroughfare. (*HIA*)

Loading American foodstuffs from the warehouse of the Commission for Polish Relief in Warsaw for delivery to children's institutions. (*HIA*)

Herbert C. Hoover during a Field Mass at Saski Square in Warsaw, August 14, 1919. Next to him (seated) is Monsignor Ratti (the papal nuncio in Poland and future Pope Pius XI) and Józef Piłsudski, chief of state. (*Hoover Institution Archives [HIA], Stanford, California*)

POLSKIE DZIECI w HOŁDZIE HOOVEROWI.

Grateful Lódź children's salute to Hoover, July 3, 1921. (*HPL*)

Foreign Minister August Zaleski and novelist Wacław Sieroszewski after unveiling of Hoover's bust in American Pavilion at Poznań World Fair, May 16, 1929. (*HPL*)

Hoover addressing the Polish-American Community for the Polish Relief Fund on Pulaski Memorial Day, October 11, 1939. (*HIA*)

Hoover before the House Foreign Affairs Committee, chaired by Rep. Sol Bloom, to present the plight of the Polish nation, February 29, 1940. (*HIA*)

Hoover listening to General Haller's address, New York City, April 28, 1940. (*HIA*)

Hoover (*center*) visiting the ruins of Warsaw Ghetto, March 1946. (*HIA*) According to Ambassador Lane, Hoover suggested: "This should be left forever as a monument to Nazi bestiality." (Arthur Bliss Lane, *I Saw Poland Betrayed: An American Ambassador Reports to the American People* [New York: Bobbs-Merrill Co., n.d.], p. 118.)

Ex-President Hoover welcomed by Warsaw children in March 1946. (Herbert Hoover, *An American Epic* [Chicago: Henry Regnery Co., 1964], vol. IV, facing p. 142.)

Documents

Documents

DOCUMENT NO. 1

Letter, MR. HOOVER *to* SIR EDWARD GREY

London, 22 December 1915

Sir,

Knowing your keen desire to mitigate in every possible way the human suffering arising out of the war, I feel justified in bringing before you a suggestion on behalf of the civil population in Poland.

I attach hereto a petition which this Commission [Commission for Relief in Belgium] has received from the large representative relief committee in Warsaw, and also the report made as the result of personal investigation, at our instance, by Dr. Vernon Kellogg, until lately director in Belgium of our work there.

No added words of mine can darken the picture of misery and despair which these statements depict, representing as they do what would have been the state of Belgium but for the relief afforded under international auspices, with your earnest support.

I have had some informal conversation with German authorities, who assured me that there are cereals and potatoes available in Poland and elsewhere, from which, by mobilisation and organised distribution, some sort of minimum ration can be provided. The other items of dietary do not exist in Poland, and they are critically necessary to preserve health to the strong, life to the weak, and to forefend from the whole population already incipient famine diseases. The shortage of these particular commodities in Germany leaves no hope of help to Poland from that quarter.

I am assured by these German authorities that protection will be afforded to local and imported supplies for the exclusive use of the civil population, also that every facility will be afforded to this Commission in its task of organisation and distribution, under proper guarantees. It appears to us that the deficient fats, beans, etc., together with condensed milk for children, can only be obtained by imports from overseas, for which there would seem to be a route practicable from the Western Hemisphere to Sweden, with transshipment thence via Danzig or Libau. We would not undertake such a task without the approval and cooperation of the Allied Governments. In the provision of food-supply for these people we should need, not only to rely on charity, but to assemble all the economic resources of Poland and its institutions, in much the same manner as has been done in Belgium; and we should need the permission of His Majesty's Government to facilitate exchange and banking operations.

The painful gravity of the situation in Poland cannot be gainsaid, nor need I apologise for the interest this organisation has taken in the Polish people, in addition to our other very grave responsibilities. We have no desire to add to our burdens, but if the fourteen months of service in Belgium have commended us to the various belligerent Governments, it is our duty to use the confidence thus acquired on behalf of the Polish people, and I wish to add that, if the Allied Governments are prepared to assent to such relief measures, and if any other institution can be summoned to undertake their execution, this Commission would be glad to give any advice arising out of its experience, or, alternatively, we should be glad to incorporate such other body in any organisation we might set up.

I have, etc.,

HERBERT HOOVER

SOURCE: Harold Henry Fisher and Sidney Brooks, *America and the New Poland* (New York: Macmillan Co., 1928), pp. 345–46.

DOCUMENT NO. 2

Plan for relief in Poland submitted to the British Government by MESSRS. HOOVER *and* WALCOTT

March 20, 1916

There are approximately 15,000,000 people in the German occupied eastern area, including Russian Poland and western Russia. Of this population, between 3,500,000 and 4,000,000 people are concentrated in, or in the immediate neighborhood of, the cities of Warsaw, Lodz, Schenzochow (Czestochowa), Vilna, Kovno and Bella Ettap (Biala Etappe).

In order to handle the problem of provisioning from a practical point of view and at the same time with proper safeguard as to all the international phases in the matter, the following basis is proposed:

(1) The American commission shall undertake the revictualing of the above mentioned cities only.

The German Government to undertake to furnish to the cities above mentioned a supply which will cover a ration of—

> 400 grams of potatoes *per diem per capita*
> 10   "   salt   "   "
> 10   "   sugar   "   "
> 3   "   tea   "   "

The American commission to import cereals to an amount which will afford a ration of 340 grams *per diem per capita* of wheat, or beans, peas, rice, maize; also with 40 grams of fats *per diem per capita* and a moderate amount of condensed milk for children.

(2) That the German Government shall undertake to revictual the whole of the balance of the population in the occupied territory.

(3) The German Government will undertake to devise financial means for the provision of gold exchange abroad to pay for the foodstuff purchased by the American commission. The Allies to give necessary permits for these financial operations by the commission.

(4) The German Government will make the necessary arrangements to turn over to the commission sufficient German shipping to do the entire transportation from North America or other places to Danzig.

(5) The revictualing to last only until October 1, at which time the new harvest will take care of the entire civilian population.

(6) The German Government to undertake that there shall be no interference with the imported foodstuffs; that they will be consumed absolutely by the native civilian population; that the American commission will be furnished every facility for the control of the entire revictualing of the cities in question, including the German contribution to the ration.

(7) In order to carry out the above it will be necessary to import approximately 40,000 tons of foodstuffs per month. It is proposed that such portion of these foodstuffs as go to the well-to-do population should be sold, and in this particular the German Government is prepared to give free railway transport

over the occupied areas and one-half railway rates over the German State railroads. It is proposed to provision the destitute without cost.

SOURCE: U.S., Department of State, "Polish Relief," in *Papers Relating to the Foreign Relations of the United States, 1916, Supplement, The World War* (Washington, D.C.: Government Printing Office, 1929), p. 889.

DOCUMENT NO. 3

Letter, MR. HOOVER *to* SECRETARY OF STATE LANSING, *asking his approval and authorization of an American Mission to Poland to study food conditions*

[Paris] December 18, 1918

The Honorable Robert Lansing
Secretary of State
Hotel de Crillon, Paris

Dear Mr. Lansing:

It is of the utmost importance that we should have some reliable information as to the food situation in Poland. The British have already sent a mission, and it seems to me vitally necessary that we should also dispatch some capable men for this purpose.

As diplomatic relations have been broken off between Poland and Germany, it seems impossible of access in that direction, the only possible manner of reaching Poland being by motor car from the Italian front, via Buda-Pesth [*sic*], thus avoiding entrance into German territory.

I am anxious to send three or perhaps four men, one being Dr. Kellogg for nutritional purposes, he being already well acquainted with Poland since the war, some transport army officer who could study transportation conditions and possibly one other American, together with an interpreter, for which latter purpose it would be useful to use Count Horodyski.

In order to accomplish this mission, I must have the delegation of two American motor cars, with drivers, from our American establishment in Italy and the assistance of the American military establishment there.

Before undertaking anything on this line, however, I need your approval and authorization to the various authorities to facilitate the movement of the mission and your request to the Commander-in-Chief that he should make the necessary dispositions in the matter.

I would be glad to know your impressions on the matter and if you approve of it, if you could take the steps above mentioned.

Faithfully yours,
HERBERT HOOVER

SOURCE: *A.R.A. Documents of the American Relief Administration European Operations, 1918–1922*, vol. 18, *Poland*, mimeographed (Stanford: Stanford University, 1932), pp. 78–79. (These volumes are available in the Hoover Institution Archives, Stanford, Calif.)

DOCUMENT NO. 4

Letter, HOOVER *to* KELLOGG, *regarding the appointment of an American Food Mission to Poland*

Paris, December 23, 1918

Dr. Vernon Kellogg
Paris

My Dear Doctor Kellogg:

In appointing you head of the United States Food Administration Polish Mission, I have but little instruction to give. I have asked Colonel Grove to accompany you to look into questions of transportation, storage and distribution, and to assist you in negotiations with regard to finance, and to take charge in Poland if we establish a permanent working relief.

Any Polish Relief at the moment, outside of public charity, will be based on securing some kind of finance which can be translated into American dollars. I am not at all sure that the Polish banks or Polish Government can develop such resources. On the other hand, they may be able, through their banks and municipalities, to effect loans in Neutral countries such as Norway and Sweden.

My idea is that you will want to first determine the need of Poland and the method through which relief could be transported and distributed. If finance can be arranged, my own view is that we should ask Colonel Grove to remain in Poland in charge of distribution in Poland, representing us in the Relief. Obviously, it is our desire in relief distribution to work through the Government so as to strengthen its hands and at the same time relieve ourselves of enormous responsibilities. The ideal arrangement would be that we should deliver cargoes at Dantzig, paid for in advance by the Polish Government; that their agents would take charge at that point, securing their transportation and distribution equitably among the populations; that Colonel Grove should, with such staff as is necessary, assure himself that the distribution was reasonably just and reasonably efficient, and conduct our relations with the Polish Government. If you can accomplish the work on this ideal, my own idea is for you personally to return to Paris to be associated with this office in the conduct of preliminary missions and investigation of need.

I wish you the best of success.

Faithfully yours,
HERBERT HOOVER

SOURCE: Suda Lorena Bane and Ralph Haswell Lutz, eds., *Organization of American Relief in Europe, 1918–1919* (Stanford: Stanford University Press, 1943), pp. 110–11.

DOCUMENT NO. 5

Letter, ALLIED SUPREME COUNCIL OF SUPPLY AND RELIEF *to* SUPREME ALLIED COMMANDER MARSHALL FERDINAND FOCH

Paris, 20th January, 1919

To Marshal Foch:

We have just heard the report of Dr. Kellogg who has completed a Mission in Poland on behalf of Mr. Hoover. It is clear from his statements that the food situation in Poland is most critical and that immediate supplies are necessary if the present Government is to be able to withstand the Bolsheviks. The Allied Supreme Council of Supply and Relief is ready to send the necessary cargoes to Dantzig at once.

Article 16 of the Armistice with Germany gives the Allies the right of access to Poland by Dantzig for the purpose of sending supplies to Poland.

We request you to ask at once by wireless that Germany should take steps to assure the transport of 300 tons of foodstuffs daily by rail from Dantzig to the Polish frontier.

The German Government must assure the protection of these supplies and should the supplies delivered in Poland prove to have been tampered with, there shall be a corresponding reduction in the future supplies for Germany.

The transport of the supplies shall be carried out under the control of Allied representatives of the Council and we request you to keep us informed by telegram.

Signed: HERBERT HOOVER   JOHN BEALE
B. ATTOLICO   CLEMENTEL

[The signatories were representatives of the United States, United Kingdom, Italy, and France in the Allied Supreme Council of Supply and Relief.]

SOURCE: Poland, A.R.A. (Paris), Hoover Institution Archives (HIA).

DOCUMENT NO. 6

Letter, HOOVER *to* GROVE

March 17, 1919

My Dear Colonel Grove:

Reports of special investigators and from many other sources confirm the existence of a very serious condition in Poland due to lack of proper food for children. All investigations indicate that in the cities and industrial centers not only is it impossible for working men and women to obtain the food which is required to maintain their children in such health as to insure growth into strong man- and woman-hood, but the mortality among these children is reported to be so large as to warrant the sympathy and active aid of the entire civilized world.

Such a situation appeals especially to the American people and therefore the American Relief Administration has established a Children's Relief Bureau at its headquarters in Paris and is prepared to assign personnel to assist the Polish Government. It proposes during the months of March, April, May and June of this year to donate $200,000 a month for this purpose in Poland. Part of this fund will come from Congressional appropriations in America. The American Relief Administration must also look to the Polish Government and the Polish people for substantial financial support, as the amount of money possible to allocate from the United States' government funds will not meet the entire needs. The money value of the American allotment, together with any funds donated for the purpose by the Polish Government will be converted into cocoa, sugar, milk, flour and perhaps certain of the fats suitable for children, which will be imported into the country by the American Relief Administration and distributed gratuitously for the purpose indicated.

Our activities in Europe are to be maintained for only a relatively short time longer; therefore it must be the constant endeavor of the American Relief Administration, after the children's relief work is organized and on a working basis, gradually to withdraw both its financial aid and its personnel and to transfer the responsibility to the Polish people to operate and maintain the work until the normal life of the country is re-established. On this account, it is preferable that the organization administering the children's relief work in Poland be officially called the Polish Children's Relief Administration or some other such name as will indicate distinctively Polish control of the work. In this manner the organization may continue to function under completely nationalized auspices.

The American Relief Administration is beginning shipments from America of cocoa, sugar, and milk, while flour and certain of the fats suitable for children have already arrived at Danzig. All these we shall donate at once free of charge. We look to the Polish Government to provide us with rail transportation for supplies from Danzig and from the various railroad stations in Poland to the points of final distribution. We must also look to the Polish people to provide the necessary facilities for supplying this food to the children, including kitchens, dining rooms, fuel and all other equipment necessary in the serving of the food.

It is believed that a Polish Children's Relief Committee should be established at once in each city and industrial center, to be composed of representative Polish men and women. These committees to be effective should be drawn from the local population and every member should actually devote personal services to the work. Committees otherwise constituted will surely lead to disaster. We will provide such experts as may be needed to assist in the work, and during the time that our activities continue, we shall exercise such supervision as we may see fit of the activities of the committees and the distribution that they make of these supplies. So far as finances will permit, the endeavor should be to furnish one meal a day to each weak and backward child. It has been found by experience that the best results are obtained by serving these meals in the various school buildings. Experience has shown that this practice means an additional inducement to the parents to keep their children at school and contributes materially to the re-establishment of normal life in the cities and industrial centers. Also there should be organized special canteens for infants, and for nursing mothers and women about to become mothers.

It is vital to act at once. Please therefore immediately take up with the Prime Minister of Poland the question of obtaining the approval of the Polish Government to the proposed plan. Explain clearly that while we will begin this work, we shall expect the full support and cooperation of the Government of Poland and the people of Poland and that we undertake no obligations to continue after August 1st, 1919.

It must be clearly explained that the existing ocean tonnage situation makes it difficult to maintain a scheduled program and we cannot therefore assume responsibility for temporary interruptions.

If all this is agreed to, you are authorized to proceed at once to cooperate with the Polish Government in establishing committees and to put the foregoing instructions into immediate effect so that these relief operations may be started as soon as the foodstuffs are available. . . .

Mr. Klotz, in his letter of March 11th, gave you the preliminary advice on this same subject. Lieut. Pate, who is now with you, has had a great deal of experience in this kind of work in Belgium and it is believed that he is thoroughly competent to supervise this work on your staff. We shall also send you such additional personnel as you may require. However, your constant effort should be to keep the American personnel down to the minimum and in purely supervisory capacities, relying upon the local Polish committees to do all of the detail work.

A detailed project of the method of your accounting for this gift will be forwarded in separate instructions.

Faithfully yours,
HERBERT HOOVER

SOURCE: William R. Grove, *War's Aftermath (Polish Relief in 1919)* (New York: House of Field, 1940), pp. 171–73.

DOCUMENT NO. 7

Letter, HOOVER *to* LANSING, *regarding the stimulation of coal production in the Duchy of Teschen*

Paris, 28 April 1919

My Dear Mr. Secretary:

With regard to the Duchy of Teschen, the Supreme Economic Council, following the precedent of Austrian railways, constituted the Director General of Relief a sort of mandatory over the coal mines in the old Austrian Empire and Poland, to secure the stimulation of production and co-ordination in distribution. The whole economic fabric of this area threatens to dissolve because of the steady decrease in coal production. The Duchy of Teschen is, of course, one of the prime sources of coal for this section, and its production has gone down to as low as 25 percent of normal.

In endeavoring to build up this situation, we are confronted at all points with the impossible political situation. I made the suggestion the other day that the question might be put in cold storage for three months if this area were put under the Director General of Relief and were conducted from a point of view of coal output rather than politics.

Mr. Paderewski would probably accept such a proposition, but I do not think the Czechs are very keen about it, as they demand the immediate solution in anticipation that such immediate action will be in their favor.

I understand the Peace Mission is anxious for any suggestion from me. I am not at all positive that this solution would work out, but, in any event, it could not be attempted unless we could have at least a couple hundred of either American or British soldiers as a police protection for the administration that we would set up. If we were dealing with it, it would be necessary to set up perhaps an Inter-Allied Commission, appointed by the Director General of Relief, this Commission to act as the de facto Government and to have such police force as above, to see that the different nationalities did not fly at each others throats. This pressure, together with the pressure of food supplies, might carry through.

Faithfully yours,
HERBERT HOOVER

SOURCE: Bane and Lutz, *Organization of American Relief,* pp. 430–31.

DOCUMENT NO. 8

Letter, HOOVER *to* WILSON, *regarding a technical advisory body for economic co-operation in Central Europe*

Paris, 24 June 1919

Dear Mr. President:

Before you leave I would like to know if I could have your informal approval to the following:

In addition to food activities, I am, under a "mandatory" given to me by the Supreme War Council, a sort of a Receiver for the whole of the railways in the Austrian Empire, and I likewise enjoy the same high office in respect to the coal mines of the Austrian Empire and Poland. There very great matters have been carried with indeed great ability by the corps of American officers whom I have had in charge in these countries. As the result of their success in maintaining economic life in this area of political dissension all enjoy a great deal of prestige with all six or eight different governments that nest around Southeastern Europe. At some moment after the signing of peace it will be necessary for us to withdraw all of these services. What these countries will want above all things will be some kind of economic inter-arrangement among themselves as to railway management, coal distribution, customs conventions, the common working of their telegraph and telephone systems, etc. I therefore have the notion that the opportunity may arise when I can go into this area and call a convention of economic delegates representing these different governments at some central point under my chairmanship, and on the ground that we were about to withdraw we should set up the preliminaries of their necessary co-operation. On this basis I have the feeling that I might produce substantial results in the solution of these vital problems.

I do not want to undertake these things without at least your approval. On the basis of simply arranging for withdrawal of our organization we will avoid jealousies of the other great governments and will, I am convinced, be able to perform a service that cannot otherwise be accomplished.

> Faithfully yours,
> HERBERT HOOVER

SOURCE: Bane and Lutz, *Organization of American Relief,* pp. 570–71.

DOCUMENT NO. 9

Letter, HOOVER *to* WILSON

Paris, June 2, 1919

My dear Mr. President:

As you are perhaps aware, there is a great agitation in the United States over the mistreatment of Jews in Poland. This agitation has been founded to some extent on misinformation. A good deal of the news that comes to the United States from Poland filters through German or Bolshevik sources. On the other hand, there has been wrong-doing and a proper illumination of it will not only act as a deterrent but will give the Polish Government an opportunity to prove its good faith.

The continuation of this agitation is likely to do the future of Poland in American estimation a great deal of harm, and I do believe that regardless of the temporary obsessions of the Polish Government for territorial aggrandizement, it must be a fundamental principle with us that we must support the Polish Republic. Therefore, in order to meet the question, I have suggested to Mr. Paderewski that he should ask you to appoint an independent committee to investigate these matters, and the Polish Government should undertake to deal out justice on any conclusions they might come to. I, of course, do not know whether you would be inclined to appoint such a commission, or not, but if so I should like to suggest that there should be on such a commission of at least four or five, at least two prominent American Jews of the broad character of Mr. Oscar Straus and Mr. Henry Morgenthau.

It might quite well be that there has been wrong-doing along the Bolshevik edge of Poland, but, on the other hand, a section of Jews in Poland have shown no support whatever to the Polish Government, and, if such a commission were wisely selected, it might not only act as a deterrent to outrages on Jews but it might also act in an advisory capacity to the Jewish community in Poland, that they should support this growing democracy as being their ultimate salvation from the tyrannies they have endured. The Polish Government is generally meeting a great deal of difficulty from the Jews in the fact that they are peculiarly subject to Bolshevik influence because of the total misery in which they have been left by the last two hundred years of mistreatment and they have also been stimulated to make trouble by the Germans, because during the war the Germans played strongly upon the past sufferings of the Jewish population as against the Poles, and many of them are rather pro-German.

This country needs moderation and good counsel on both sides of this problem.

Yours faithfully,
HERBERT HOOVER

SOURCE: Poland, A.R.A. (Paris), HIA.

DOCUMENT NO. 10

Letter, HOOVER *to* GENERAL PERSHING, *requesting the appointment of Colonel Gilchrist on the Polish Typhus Mission*

June 27th, 1919

General J. J. Pershing
Commander-in-Chief
American Expeditionary Forces
Paris, France

My Dear General Pershing,

Central Europe is now in the initial ravages of an epidemic of typhus that must be checked during this summer or it will lead to an appalling destruction of life next winter. The Red Cross section of the League of Nations is not yet organized. Poland, where the epidemic is at its worst, does not possess the material equipment or the trained personnel necessary to eradicate the disease during the summer by adequate disinfection of the population. The disinfection equipment the Polish Government is purchasing from the Liquidation Boards of the Allied Armies. The American Army has been freed of infestation by vermin through the activity of a special service organized for this work. At the present time this organization is about to be broken up and its members returned to the United States, where there is no need for this special service. The officer who has been in charge of this work, Colonel H. L. Gilchrist, has completed his work in France. I know of no way in which our sympathy for the distressed peoples of Central Europe can be better expressed than in the transfer of American officers to this service for temporary duty. Since it is my understanding that the President alone has the authority to detail an American officer to a foreign country, this matter has been laid before the President, who has given his approval to the project in the form of a communication addressed to yourself, which is enclosed herewith. It involves not to exceed a dozen officers for three or four months. We possess trustworthy surveys of the situation in Poland and know that these officers would accomplish an enormous service for good in that country during the next few months. In emphasizing the great importance of this mission, I beg to request that you authorize the transfer of Colonel Gilchrist and his trained personnel for temporary duty in Poland.

Believe me,
Faithfully yours,
HERBERT HOOVER

SOURCE: Bane and Lutz, *Organization of American Relief,* pp. 579–80.

DOCUMENT NO. 11

Cablegram, HOOVER *to* SECRETARY OF WAR BAKER

Paris, July 11, 1919

Honorable Newton D. Baker
Secretary of War

Epidemic of typhus in Poland can only be solved by aid of United States. Our Army has special disinfectation equipment no longer needed in France. On approval of the President General Pershing has ordered the officers detailed to Poland for a few months to cooperate with Polish Government. The

Army has sold to the Polish Government a portion of the equipment not feasible for return to the United States. Usefulness of officers and equipment will be nil unless trained enlisted men belonging to this particular service are also detailed to Poland. Since the Commanding General has no power to detail enlisted men which lies in the hands of the Secretary of War, we urge for the sake of a most important international work that you issue orders detailing to Poland the trained enlisted men now serving under Colonel H. L. Gilchrist in France. This plan in aid of Poland was discussed with the President and has his approval. It would be possible to secure that these men volunteer for the service if they can be kept on the army payroll.

HOOVER

SOURCE: *A.R.A. Documents of the American Relief Administration European Operations, 1918–1922,* vol. 19, *Poland, Typhus Relief,* mimeographed (Stanford: Stanford University, 1932), p. 442.

DOCUMENT NO. 12

Memorandum prepared by the Director General of Relief for submission to the Council of Five

July 26, 1919

REPATRIATION OF PRISONERS OF WAR
FROM SIBERIA AND ELSEWHERE

It appears that there are some 200,000 German-Austrian and Hungarian prisoners in Siberia, and that these prisoners are suffering greatly and are a constant menace to the Siberian Government. There are also certain Polish prisoners and civilians now scattered all over the world who will require more systematic assistance at repatriation, but there is an entire deficiency of funds with which to pay the incidental expenses. There are probably also other odd lots of expatriates of various nationals as the result of the war, who need systematic repatriation. It would appear to me that this problem requires definite organization, and I should like to submit the following plan in the matter for action by the Council.

First, that a Commission, comprising a British, French, American and Italian military officer, should be set up and undertake the management of this repatriation. That this Commission should communicate their appointment to the Austrian, Hungarian and Polish and other Governments, and that they should offer to undertake the repatriation, provided funds are placed to their credit in advance by each of the Governments concerned.

It would appear to me that if such a body is set up under capable officers that they would be able to work out a solution in this manner and to secure from the Allied Governments the necessary shipping and other services which would be necessary. They could invite a delegate of each of the Governments concerned to sit with them in respect to the matters which concerned such a Government and they could engage the necessary staff to carry on the work. They would probably need to appeal to the various Allied Governments and to charitable societies for some assistance in respect to prisoners originating from quarters unable to supply those funds, but, in any event, they would create a center around which all effort of this kind could be directed.

With the repatriation of the Allied troops nearing completion, it would appear to be an appropriate moment for the erection of such a body. I attach two memoranda on the subject indicating the volume of the problem involved, the first from the British Authorities on "Prisoners in Siberia", the second from the Polish Office for Repatriation.

HERBERT HOOVER.

SOURCE: *A.R.A. Bulletin* (Paris), ser. 1, vol. 2, no. 21 (August 8, 1919): 11–12.

DOCUMENT NO. 13

Report, HOOVER *to* WARSAW, *1919*

REPORT OF THE AMERICAN RELIEF ADMINISTRATION
EUROPEAN CHILDREN'S FUND MISSION TO POLAND

Reports from special inspectors, as well as information received from other sources, confirm the belief that conditions in Poland, caused by the lack of food, are deplorable. Investigation shows that in towns and industrial localities workmen cannot obtain food for their children, and that mortality among them is so great that the whole civilized world is filled with compassion and a desire to actively assist.

These terrible conditions appeal especially to the American nation, and the American Relief Administration has therefore opened a children's relief bureau to help the Polish Government in this great relief work.

The American Relief Administration expects that the Polish Government, as well as the whole nation, will help it in this action, as the money of the United States will not be sufficient to avert the misery. American subscriptions, together with the contributions and support of the Polish Government, will purchase cocoa, sugar, milk, rice, peas, and fats. These foodstuffs will be imported to Poland by the A.R.A. and distributed among needy children.

We expect the Polish Government to transport these provisions by rail from Danzig, or other railway stations, to the distribution points. We also expect to be helped by the Polish people in the conveying of this food to the children.

SOURCE: *Report of the American Relief Administration European Children's Fund Mission to Poland* (Warsaw: A.R.A., 1922), p. 8.

DOCUMENT NO. 14

Hoover address at Paderewski Dinner

Warsaw, August 13, 1919

This is my first visit to Poland since 1914. I had been many times in Warsaw before that time and always left the city with a sense of profound depression at the misery of people and the apparent hopelessness of their rightful aspirations.

In consequence, the most dramatic event that I have ever witnessed was the review of Polish troops, with Polish officers marching through the streets of Warsaw, with the old Russian Church in the back-ground.

Poland in eight months has shown the most astonishing ability at political government. A nation has been created, and it has been armed. Order has been established and maintained; the foundation has been laid for economic government.

As head of the Supreme Economic Council, I have had an unusual opportunity to observe the progress of economic restoration and the economic currents that now dominate the world, and I am daily impressed with the fact that while political government can be established in a period of days, and armies created and order restored in a period of months, yet economic recuperation cannot take place, much less economic government built up, short of years.

Poland has accomplished the first essentials of government; she has secured her liberty and armed herself against external enemies, and has built up political solidarity and restored order.

Now she has before her the greatest task of all, that is, the upbuilding of her economic life. This is nine-tenths a problem domestic to Poland herself. External aid by way of supplies and finance is a small portion of the entire problem. In the economic situation of the world today, with shortages of supplies due to five years of destruction, with shortages of capital, with economic depression throughout the world, Poland must look even more to her own resources than would be the case if the rest of the world were not itself engaged on these same problems and suffering from the same economic disorganization. The next year for all the world will be a year of tightening the belt, no less for Poland than for all other countries. It will be a year in which sould [*sic*] government must insist on the maximum production of every useful commodity, upon the utmost economy in the expenditure of *every* commodity, and upon the elimination of every non-essential that is possible. Poland must have certain supplies from abroad. Ultimately she must pay for these supplies by the shipment of commodities in exchange, and the quicker that Poland can begin to produce commodities for export the quicker will prosperity and a higher standard of living come to her people. By prohibiting the import of non-essentials, by stimulating production at every quarter, by economy in every commodity, it should not require a great length of time to put Poland on the high road to recovery, and the sole end of all this is simply to attain a constantly higher standard of living of the whole people—and this is the object of all good government.

These things can only be accomplished by sheer labor,—the co-ordinated labor of hands and of brains, and those who labor with their hands have as much responsibility in this matter as those who labor with their brains. There is no royal road to a high standard of living. The Bolshevists of Russia have thought that the road lay along their path and every reading man in Poland knows that the Bolsheviks have brought starvation to their people through sheer cessation of production in a country that formerly had a surplus for export. The production of coal, food, and every commodity is just as important to the future of Poland today as has been the sacrifice of lives on her frontiers. It is much harder and much less glorious to live for the State than to die for it. It is a magnificent thing to sacrifice one's life for an ideal, but the patience and the strength required from both labor and brains for Poland during the next year will be the test of the Polish people's willingness to live for an ideal.

The world is wondering whether Poland has sufficient patience and sacrifice to accomplish this, the hardest of all problems.

The setting up of economic government and the restoration of economic life can only be accomplished with time and infinite patience. Due to the oppression of Poland during the last one hundred years and fifty, there has been no opportunity to develop that mass of men skilled in economic administration, out of which governmental departments can be built. Poland must develop these men coincidently with the development of economic life; therefore hers is a double problem and requires double patience.

There is one criticism made of Poland that is really not a criticism; it is an expression of sympathy. The Polish people, under the oppression they have suffered these hundred and fifty years, have been resolute in opposition to all governments that have been imposed upon them. They have learned the sense of political opposition as no other people have learned it, and it has brought them their freedom. But to learn the sense of political support to government, of political encouragement, to endeavor on the part of the Government, and the presumption that the Government now belongs to the Polish People, is Poland's present greatest difficulty. Herein lies the patience of the Polish people. The question is whether the Polish people have the patience and strength to sit in the midst of these tremendous problems and economic difficulties and to solve them without a swing to extreme radicalism on one side with the inevitable misery and ultimate swing to reaction on the other. No government can swing to extreme radicalism and back to reaction without the most fearful misery, loss of life, delay in national progress, and even political jeopardy. The liberalism of the entire world will for generations be influenced by the success of the Polish people as its exponents.

Liberalism is youth; it requires the spirit and vigor of youth; Poland has youth and she must give her young men a chance.

Liberalism is an ideal; reaction and extreme radicalism are sheer selfishness. That idealism of the Polish people that has survived these terrible one hundred and fifty years should carry her through the next two years to economic safety.

SOURCE: Poland, A.R.A (London), HIA.

DOCUMENT NO. 15

Hoover address at Lwów City Hall

August 15, 1919

. . . These are serious times for all serious men, and our thoughts therefore must necessarily turn to serious questions. Since coming to Warsaw I had felt a certain air of discouragement in some of the higher officials of the government over the stupendous social and economic problems with which Poland is faced.

I feel, on the other hand, extremely optimistic. I know that the men who are engaged in weaving a tapestry often see only the weakness of the threads and the mistakes in the warp. I have enjoyed, however, the privilege for the last seven months of viewing the Polish problems daily, but from afar, and in my vision I have seen the gradual weaving of a great masterpiece of human liberty. We have only to consider that the freedom of Poland was suddenly erected eight months ago out of the sudden defeat of Germany. Here lay a new State embracing thirty millions of people, covering a territory ravaged by the invasion of armies; robbed of the food for its population; its industrial life demolished; its railroads denuded of rolling stock; its communications cut off from the outside world; with no access to the sea; the people so impoverished that even the name of a budget was scarcely possible. Beyond all this, and after one hundred and fifty years of tyranny, faced with the necessity of raising a modern government with all its complexities, and creating this government with minds and hands utterly unaccustomed to the functions and routine of government, today we find the Polish State consolidated politically, its independence welcome in the family of nations, with internal order restored, with a victorious and well organized army of one half million men protecting her frontiers, with the foundations laid not only for the economic revival of the country, but also for the first time in the history of Poland, political departments functioning and devoted to the welfare and upbuilding of the spiritual and intellectual side of the people. Is there room here for discouragement? Was ever so great an accomplishment in government before? In the erection of this government, the Polish people have chosen for themselves the hardest path of government, but they have chosen the only path that leads to the ultimate well-being and true liberty of her people. They have chosen the path of democracy, with the stern resolution to erect a government for the people by the people. Under these terrible circumstances, it might have been easier to create a tyranny and by the rule of a dictator and blood to solve many problems more rapidly, but the course chosen by the Poles is the only road that leads to internal liberty. In the choice of representative government, Poland has determined upon the Government of liberalism, a government midway between reaction and extreme radicalism. It is the path of idealism, and it can only be maintained by the leadership of idealists. Poland is fortunate in having in her leadership two out of the six or seven great idealist statesmen of the world, Mr. Pilsudski and Mr. Paderewski. Upon them the eyes of all liberals in all countries are today turned with hopes for their continued success. The helping hand of all liberal governments will be extended to these men and to the Polish people in the consummation of their task.

The problems yet to be solved in Poland are so enormous as to appall the courage of even the greatest idealists. They can be solved; but they can only be solved by time and patience. There is no royal road to liberty. To create the independence and liberty of the state itself is even an easier task than to create true liberty within the state. A people who have been repressed by one hundred and fifty years of tyranny, whose every aspiration and hope for progress has been stifled, a people who are trained only in the fine art of political opposition will find the task one filled with discouragement. But no man can say that a people who have maintained a hundred and fifty years of steady opposition to tyranny have not within themselves that idealism and that patience out of which true liberty can be built.

I know I breathe the earnest prayer of the whole one hundred and ten million people in the United States for the success of the Polish democracy and the confidence which they hold that true liberty has now come to Poland.

SOURCE: Poland, A.R.A. (London), HIA.

DOCUMENT NO. 16

Hoover address at Polish Convention

Buffalo, November 12, 1919

I have been asked to speak to you on the program which has been made with the establishment of free government of the Polish people: Of the service that you can do in the maintenance of this inspiring Republic: Of the service that you must maintain at the same time to the country of your adoption.

I have had the fortune to be associated since 1914 with many of the men who are now comprised in the government of Poland. More particularly, since last January I have been in intimate association with the problem and perplexities of the Polish people. It is truly an inspiring thing to witness thirty millions of people of one race and one language emerge from 150 years of foreign military dictatorship into a free country. It is doubly inspiring to an American to see a new nation founded on the inspiration and ideals that we of the United States hold as the very basis of liberty.

The sympathies of the American and Polish peoples are not an over-night creation. There is not a school child of the United States who does not know of the great service to our war for freedom through those great military leaders, Kosciusko and Pulaski. There is not a Pole who does not know the service these same men gave to free Poland, for which they gave their lives. Further, during this 150 years there has been a constant migration of Poles to the United States in an endeavor to find freedom. There has been a constant return of these Poles to Poland and an interpretation of American hopes and ideals amongst the Polish people. The American sympathy for the struggle of Poland to secure her independence has been constant from the days of our own freedom. It was President Wilson who first enunciated the absolute stipulation that the complete independence of the whole of the Polish people was a fundamental condition of this peace.

You, the Polish citizens of the United States, have out of sympathy for your mother country been constant in contribution and moral support to these leaders for Polish independence who entered Warsaw in triumph in January this year. You have contributed not only your resources but your sons to this great thing. America has still another great link of sympathy with Poland. One of those two great Poles who now lead the Polish people lived many years in the United States and his inspiration and vision of government arise from our institutions. . . . One of the two great men who have been the builders of the freedom of Poland is practically an American citizen. These two great men, Paderewski and Pilsudski, are today two of the greatest figures that have emerged from this war. They have the abilities, the courage and resolution of constructive statesmanship.

It requires but a short review of the situation that existed ten months [ago] within the present boundaries of Poland in contrast to its position today to appreciate the gigantic strides of the independence of Poland. Poland has been for 150 years under subjugation of foreign military government. The Polish people were given no opportunity for the development of political experience. Their only training as statesmen lay in political sabotage and in opposition. This same opposition has maintained alive the spirit of Poland for over 150 years and, ripening at time into bloody revolution, finally secured the Polish people their independence. Yet political opposition is a poor school for constructive government. The world feared that the Poles would fall in this emergency—but they have not.

During the war Poland has been ravaged by four separate invasions— parts of it by even seven invasions. The destruction of property and civilian life was greater than all the destruction of property and life on the Western front. Between three and four millions of Poles had died of starvation or disease during the war. The Russians had ruthlessly destroyed thousands of square miles and driven the entire population from home in an endeavor to create a desert that might retard the advance of the German armies. This shocking barbarity, the literally hundreds of thousands who died as refugees at the roadsides, is itself perhaps one of the curses that fell on the military oligarchy of Russia. The Germans also systematically abstracted at the point of the bayonet every resource of Poland, scraping away such minor surpluses of food as existed in the more prolific sections of Poland and leaving other regions to starve. This, together with the destruction of her farms and the looting of every bit of agricultural machinery, left millions of Poles at the

Armistice threatened with starvation. There is a greater exhaustion of work animals in Poland than in any other part of Europe.

At the time of the Armistice, approximately one quarter of Poland was in the hands of the Austrian army, approximately one half in the hands of the German army, something over one quarter in the hands of the Bolshevik army. The Armistice called for the evacuation of certain undoubted Polish territory by the German and Austrian armies. With the German withdrawal, hordes of Bolsheviks invaded a large part of Poland, perpetrating indescribable crimes in every village and city. Even in the East, North and South, the Armistice provisions left Poland completely surrounded with enemy territory. She had no outlet to the sea and could not send a letter or a telegram except through enemy hands. I do not know in history of so appalling and disheartening a situation as faced that great soldier and patriot, Pilsudski, when, escaped from a German prison, he laid the first stone of the Polish Government at Warsaw. Here was a country of thirty million people in a state of total anarchy: In the midst of a famine such that the children had ceased to play upon the streets; a country with thousands dying daily from Typhus and contagious diseases; a large part of the country in the terrible grip of Bolshevik invasion; the Bolshevik army advancing behind a cloud of conspirators, and disintegrated by 150 years of separation, a population incapable of paying taxation; a people absolutely without the means for preserving order or repelling invasion; a people without even the rudimentary machinery on which to build a great administrative government. The railways and telegraph lines had been greatly destroyed and had practically ceased to function. The rolling stock had been destroyed or removed from the country.

Yet, eight months after the arrival of Pilsudski in Warsaw, I found in Poland a vigorous government, functioning with Ministries of Foreign Affairs, of War, of Food, of Finance, of Railways, of Labor, of Education, of Agriculture and of Public Health. An army of 500,000 well-drilled, well-equipped and spirited troops. Order established throughout the entire area. The Bolsheviki driven out of Poland. A general election had taken place under universal franchise. A congress had been set up, and from the moment that it convened the government of Poland ruled, responsible to this assembly. Local government had been established in every quarter. Land reform had been inaugurated by law. A public school system had been established. Poland, after ten months, was a democracy with a government for the people and by the people, in a country that had had no government for 150 years but government of foreign oppression. Railways had been rebuilt. Abandoned cars and locomotives had been repaired and brought into use. Regular, though deficient, train services were being maintained over 30,000 miles of railways. Canals were opened and in operation. Coal mines were running. Fields abandoned for years were being steadily replanted. Post and telegraph services had been re-established. Typhus was being brought under control. The fundamental finance of government was being steadily extended. Poland had gained at the Peace Conference her critically necessary boundaries and her outlet to the sea. The people had been fed, and children were again playing in the streets.

I am proud that the United States could have had, through her organized representatives in Poland, a material part in the making of this great miracle. I am proud to have been appointed by the American government to direct this service. American assistance was given to Poland in ships, in opening the route to the sea through Danzig, in railway material and skill, in fighting famine and typhus, in financial assistance to the Government, in charity to the poor. Beyond this, devoted and disinterested Americans had participated in the building of her economic and political government. This service marks the final repayment of a debt of the American people of 150 years' standing.

The need of Poland for help and assistance from the United States is not yet over. That assistance must continue for yet another year. In another year Poland will have found herself not only with fully developed political institutions but her great resources will give her an economic independence that will enable her to contribute to the welfare of others. Owing to the destruction of agriculture, it will be another year before Poland will be able to produce sufficient food to maintain her population. Fully thirty percent of the fertile land of Eastern Poland has as yet no plows. Her railways require more reconstruction and more rolling stock. Her spinning mills must be repaired and raw material found for their operation. Six hundred thousand workmen are idle, because they have not the material on which to labor. Five years, with literally no production or imports of textiles, have left the Polish people underclad and cold. Typhus still rages on her Eastern frontiers. Her population is as yet unable to contribute in taxes the necessary expenditures of the Government. Her currency was inflated and debauched by enemy armies by every device known to financial robbery, and, above all, Poland today must hold the front line of Europe against Bolshevik invasion. In the midst of her economic misery, she must maintain an army of 500,000 men, fighting on a front of 1500 miles, as the outpost of Europe. Yet the people of Poland are fired by an emotion of freedom and sacrifice that will carry her over another year of suffering. A little help will mitigate that suffering, will expedite her recovery, will guarantee the final stability of her free institutions.

The Polish Government has been confronted with a most difficult problem in the matter of its large Jewish population. These people have suffered from the same terrible domination as the Poles themselves. They have been driven from the proper development of participation in all branches of agriculture and industrial and intellectual life into the narrow froove [*sic*] of middle-men, and held there in the most terrible submersion.

The result is, more especially in times of famine when the middle-man of any kind is between the upper and nether mill stone, that racial conflict has been heightened.

Whatever the qualities of the Jewish people of Poland may be, in the minds of their critics it must be borne in mind that their present position is the doing of the Gentile and all the world has yet to pay for this accumulated century of injustice. For this, the Polish Government now ten months old is not responsible. With a government gradually developing stability with law and order, the latent animosities of populations escape to the surface. It is not my intention to traverse what may or may not have happened in Poland, but only to point out that in a period of ten months the Polish Government has developed to a point that life is safe and that freedom from tyranny is accomplished. The fine, non-sectarian work done by the Jewish Joint Distribution Committee for Poland and the active leadership of many important Poles and Jews in finding a solution to this accumulation of centuries of wrong, have placed the whole Jewish problem on a new footing, and one to which we have every reason to look forward with confidence.

Thus, the coming winter will be a hard winter in Poland. It will not be so hard as the winter that we have passed, and how hard it will be will depend entirely upon the service that Poland can secure from the United States. Poland requires six or eight hundred thousand tons of wheat and rye. She requires 100,000 tons of fats. She ought to have 200,000 bales of cotton. She also requires other raw materials. Altogether, the economic life of Poland could be kept revolving and her position steadily improved if she could find credits for $150,000,000 in the United States. I believe it is the duty of the Poles themselves to directly organize this assistance and to prevent any fishing by intermediaries for a profit in this pool of misery. You should have a strongly developed organization that will scrutinize the appeals made to you.

Poland requires charity for her destitute. I and my colleagues are endeavoring to provide the food supply and clothing for 1,200,000 destitute, undernourished Polish children. Committees comprising the most devoted Polish men and women have been established in every city and village in Poland. Canteens for feeding children have been in operation for many months. They were established by the American Government, but their appropriations have been exhausted; they must now depend upon charity. These are the two problems before the Poles in the United States, as to whether you in the greater prosperity that you enjoy, are prepared to devote your major resources to the loaning of money to the Government of Poland for the purchases of its essentials, and whether you are prepared to assist us in charity in the support of your own brothers and sisters in Poland who are preserving the life of 1,200,000 children. The Polish Government and public charity are paying all the expenses of this organization in Poland. We are depending upon you to enable us to buy in the United States the clothes, milk and other foods for those children, which cannot be bought in Poland.

There is another subject on which I wish to say a few words, and that is the question of the duties of citizenship of Poles in the United States. You and your ancestors have come to the United States to free yourselves from oppression and to participate in a country of greater prosperity and a higher standard of living. You have come, therefore, to take advantage of the institutions that have been built up here in 150 years for the well-being of the people in this country. You have been given the privilege of entrance into this country without restriction and you have benefited by its blessings. It is right that you should have a tender heart for the country of your origin, but your first and primary duty is to the country of your adoption. It is a happy circumstance that the whole of the American people are equally anxious with citizens of Polish origin for the upbuilding of the Polish Republic, and that therefore there is no conflict in this service to both countries.

The people of the United States are today themselves facing great difficulties of social and industrial character. If we are to solve these difficulties, it will be by the undivided support of our institutions from which we have obtained the blessings which we now enjoy. Many foolish ideas are being circulated amongst the foreign-born population of the United States. Many of these foreign-born are interesting themselves in the destruction of our primary institutions and defiance of our laws. The American people are fast losing patience with this attitude. It may develop out of this that the "open door" toward Europe will be in a large measure closed. But, worse than this, there may develop out of it a prejudice against every speaker of a foreign language in the United States. It creates prejudice against extending aid to those countries in Europe from which our foreign-born populations spring.

If reforms are needed in the United States, they will be carried out by those whose parents have grown up amidst our institutions and those who have become in sentiment and spirit a part of our people. It is fortunate that the Polish population of the United States have been but little influenced by these forms of agitation. If a Pole exists who has associated himself with the organizations that devote themselves to the destruction of our institutions, that Pole is not only disloyal to the United States, but he is endeavoring to paralyze the arm that is supporting the independence of his own mother country. Those who are dissatisfied with our institutions can always choose the alternative of retiring to those from which they came.

It is therefore the duty of those of you who speak our language and who have lived under our institutions, to see to it that people of your blood do not associate themselves with movements that are antagonistic to our public sentiment and to our social and economic institutions.

HERBERT HOOVER

SOURCE: *For Relief in Poland: Address of Herbert Hoover before the Polish Convention* (Chicago: National Polish Committee of America, 1919).

DOCUMENT NO. 17

Letter, HOOVER *to* ANNA BADURA

October 11, 1922

Miss Anna Badura
c/o The Young Womens Christian Association
600 Lexington Avenue, New York City

My dear Miss Badura:

Now that your work in Poland is completed it seems opportune to voice the appreciation of my associates in the American Relief Administration and myself for the splendid contribution of the Polish Administration in Poland. That the successful accomplishment of this important humanitarian work was due in no inconsiderable measure to the resource and activity of yourself and the other young women of your unit, is a fact which I find pleasure in recording.

It will not soon be forgotten that much of this work was necessarily performed under conditions of physical hardship, if not personal risk, and it is most gratifying to reflect that the message of American assistance to the unfortunate people of Poland was carried by the Gray Samaritans in a spirit of utter unselfishness and with that sympathetic understanding so essential in a benevolent enterprise. Poland was indeed fortunate, during the critical period of starvation, in having the children of her own sons and daughters as ambassadors of mercy from the republic in which they had taken up their homes.

Faithfully yours,
HERBERT HOOVER

SOURCE: Polish Gray Samaritans, HIA.

DOCUMENT NO.18

Letter, HOOVER *to the* CHILDREN OF POLAND

December 8, 1921

To the children of Poland:

I am deeply grateful for the beautiful albums, scrolls and long lists of autographs that you have sent me in token of your understanding of the friendship shown you by the American people through the years of Poland's struggle since the Armistice.

As Chairman of the American Relief Administration, I thank you on behalf of the organization as a whole, and especially in the name of those devoted Americans, members of the American Relief Administration, who have journeyed into your country and served faithfully that you might be helped to grow into robust and happy citizens. I hope that the work we have been able to do among you may help to build up in you those ideals of freedom and civilization for which America entered the Great War.

Yours faithfully,
HERBERT HOOVER

SOURCE: Degrees and Other Honors, Commerce Papers, Hoover Presidential Library (HPL), West Branch, Iowa.

DOCUMENT NO. 19

Telegram, HOOVER *to* BARBER *and* DURAND

February 2, 1921

. . . First: Am not prepared undertake appeal American public charity breadstuffs for adult population Poland unless am officially requested to do so in name people Poland by Chief State and Prime Minister. Consider such course by Poland would infinitely injure her credit and standing as nation and have no assurance that the response would be sufficient. On the other hand we shall undertake the feeding of one and one half million children to degree necessary to maintain them in health. Second: Failure of Polish financial relations with the United States dates back to unwillingness Polish Government in winter of nineteen nineteen to accept my recommendation for complete control of remittances and setting up adequate financial agencies United States. Am informed by American banks remittances have since that time exceeded hundred million dollars. Value of those remittances for purchasing purposes has been totally dissipated by filtration through German and Allied banks and fraudulent practices. Have repeatedly insisted that this was not only important avenue of national income to Poland but that it formed sound basis for bank advances in the United States. Have repeatedly advised all Polish representatives Adamski, Rybarski and Lubomirski at different times that if they would organise this business through some American banking group acting on behalf of Polish Government or the Polish State Bank that they could finance their bread-stuffs. Also protested at the use of monies raised on Polish loan in United States for purposes other than purchase of food. If the plan drawn by Rybar-ski for centralising Polish remittances through Guaranty Trust Company, New York had been carried out at time that I again laid the foundation for him months ago you would not be in present situation. Polish agents in spite of repeated appeals are unable to secure any authority to complete this con-tract. If this contract were closed today would result in provision of some finance for Poland and might accomplish at least one half of your problem. I am advised that delay is due to plans of Adamski to engage private Polish banks for a profit purpose. If Polish Government wishes to secure American financial assistance it should at once empower Arct or Lubomirski to close negotiation for centralising remittances it should prohibit the entrance of remittances into Poland on any other terms than through Government or the State Bank acting with the Guaranty Trust or some other bank here and it should be prepared to offer first mortgage on the railways of Poland as further security for an advance of ten or fifteen million dollars for twelve months loan. Inasmuch as I am convinced that it is only total incompetence of the Polish financial policy that results in the starvation of Polish people I have little desire to charge this incompetency to American charity. Fourth*: Any advances from the United States Government either by appropriation or from the War Finance Corporation are totally infeasible as they are fully aware of above and our Government has already carried the burden of Polish food for two years in the face of failure of Polish financial authori-ties to make adequate arrangements in their own interest. New foreign trade financing corporation will not be in business for another sixty days and even when it begins will require centralisation of remittances and some prior charges on securities such as Polish railways as a foundation for any nego-tation. If any sound reasons have been advanced against my suggestions I have yet to hear them. Finally no one regrets the suffering of the dangers to Polish situation as much as I but it is certainly absolutely useless to call upon me for help when my advice in intimate contact as I am with the whole of the financial possibilities of the United States has been disregarded not once but continually by the Polish Finance Ministry over the last two years.

*Either the third point is missing from the original telegram, or it should be "Third" instead of "Fourth."

SOURCE: Halina Janowska and Czesław Madajczyk, eds., *Archiwum polityczne Ignacego Paderewskiego* (Wrocław: Ossolineum, 1974), 2: 627–29.

DOCUMENT NO. 20

TOTAL NUMBER CHILDREN AND NURSING MOTHERS FED, MONTH BY MONTH, FROM BEGINNING OF OPERATIONS TO AUGUST 1, 1922

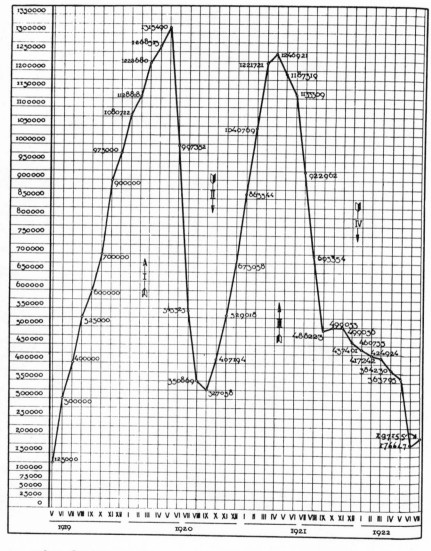

SOURCE: Frank M. Surface and Raymond L. Bland, *American Food in the World War and Reconstruction Period: Operations of the Organizations under the Direction of Herbert Hoover, 1914–1924* (Stanford: Stanford University Press, 1931), p. 230.

DOCUMENT NO. 21

Map of Poland showing principal warehouses and cities where A.R.A. carried on child-feeding operations

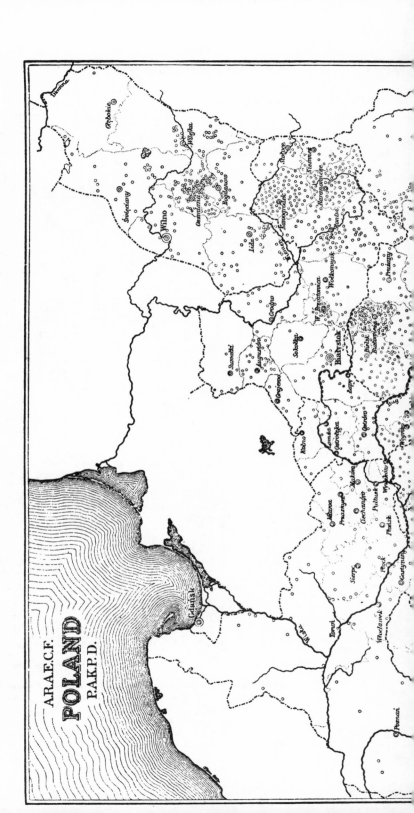

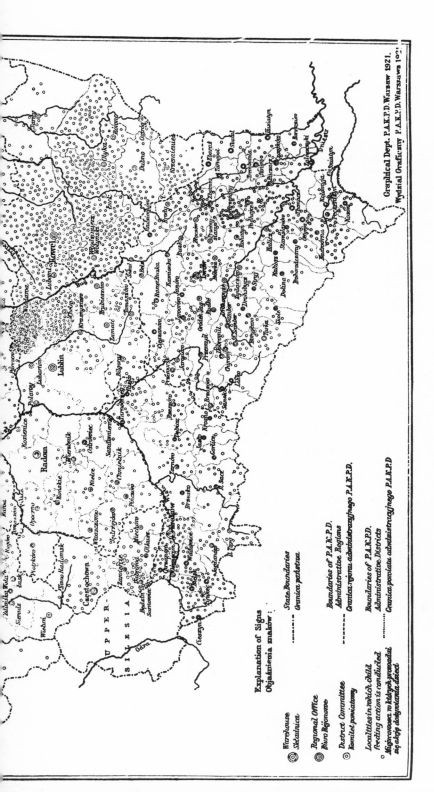

SOURCE: Frank M. Surface and Raymond L. Bland, *American Food in the World War and Reconstruction Period: Operations of the Organizations under the Direction of Herbert Hoover, 1914–1924* (Stanford: Stanford University Press, 1931), p. 749. See also *America and the New Poland*, p. 214.

DOCUMENT NO. 22

SUMMARY OF TOTAL RELIEF DELIVERIES TO POLAND

Operation	Total Metric Tons	Total Value
Armistice Period		
American Relief Administration (Congressional Appropriation)	260,843.2	$ 63,191,316.61
American Relief Administration (freight finance)	. .	544,035.40
U.S. Liquidation Commission	107,126.0	59,365,111.97
Jewish Joint Distribution Committee	9,705.8	3,412,497.00
American Red Cross	4,042.6	813,800.00
Total from United States	381,717.6	$127,326,760.98
United Kingdom (commodities)	21,462.0	$ 6,304,620.00
United Kingdom (freight finance)	. .	1,389,920.00
Polish League of Women	4.1	1,640.00
Russo-Carpathian Commission	.5	200.00
Total other than United States	21,466.6	$ 7,696,380.08
Total, Armistice Period	403,184.2	$135,023,140.98
Reconstruction Period		
American Relief Administration (Congressional Appropriation)	16,700.9	$ 6,055,842.03
European Children's Fund	59,242.5	16,769,322.10
Polish Government donation	44,569.9	6,702,221.02
Other Polish donations	1,040.9	40,094.51
Jewish Joint Distribution Committee	537.0	273,555.00
Total children's relief	122,091.2	$ 29,841,034.66
A.R.A. Warehouses (food drafts and bulk sales)	7,839.5	$ 1,675,087.41
A.R.A. Warehouses (Danzig sale to Polish Government)	7,720.3	864,562.40
Polish Government donation (adult relief)	7,072.7	917,059.24
The Commonwealth Fund (intelligentsia clothing)	30.4	57,532.49
American Friends Service Committee	633.3	30,291.26
U.S. Grain Corporation (Act of Congress, March 30, 1920)	202,564.0	24,353,590.97
United Kingdom (freight finance)	. .	8,102,558.32
Total other than children's relief	225,861.2	$ 36,000,682.09
Total, Reconstruction Period	347,951.4	$ 65,841,716.75
Grand total relief deliveries	751,135.6	$200,864,857.73

SOURCE: Surface and Bland, *American Food,* p. 226.

DOCUMENT NO. 23

Personnel

P. B. Allen
Frank Baackes
James H. Becker
A. H. Bergstrom
L. A. Blackwell
John R. Bolin
Shade H. Booth
W. duB. Brookings
Allen M. Butler
Roscoe C. Butler
Thos. V. Coleman
Merian C. Cooper
Stuart L. Craig
Capt. Czaja
Anthony Czarniecki
Paul Deisler
Milburn Doss
H. L. Dunn
George E. Duran
J. D. Ellis
Norman French
August Gerber
John S. Gratowski
William R. Grove
David C. Hanrahan
George P. Harrington
David R. Hawkins

Arthur H. Hegstrom
John B. Hollister
Joseph Houseworth
Wallace Johnson
John Kaminski
James J. Kann
Vernon Kellogg
Edward H. Kinn
Alan T. Klots
Rudolph Kock
Leon Kozakiewicz
Joseph Kropernicki
Robert Funz
John H. Lange
Chauncey McCormick
Arthur D. Mayer
Lucian E. Messinger
Harlan S. Miller
C. A. Moses
A. B. Montfort
Charles E. Neave
Bertrand Neidecker
Wm. R. Nellegar
F. H. Newberry
Albert P. Newhart
Arnold G. Nielson
Frank Nowak

Maurice Pate
William E. Perry
Glenn M. Pike
Edward J. Prebis
Harry Ratner
Lloyd R. Reynolds
Henry M. Rees
Lloyd R. Riggs
Nathan Rosen
Jacob Rosenfeld
Frank K. Ross
Thos. R. Ryan
George M. Selden
F. E. Slack
Harwood Stacy
James O. Taylor
Reginald R. Tooley
John N. Trierweiler
John C. Ulrick
Eugene O. Walker
Barclay H. Warburton
James W. Webb
A. D. Whittemore
Henry Witt
Chas. A. Wikle, Jr.

A. B. Barber
R. N. Ferguson
A. J. Fisk
H. R. Gabriel

C. S. Gaskill
W. E. Joyce
James A. Logan
William B. Poland

Edgar Rickard
T. R. Ryan
H. B. Smith

SOURCE: Grove, *War's Aftermath*, p. 219.

DOCUMENT NO. 24

Personnel

AMERICAN RELIEF ADMINISTRATION
CONNECTED WITH POLISH RELIEF AND RECONSTRUCTION
1919–1923

Robert W. Anstey	William N. Gwynn	Maurice Pate
Constance Baker	Perrin C. Galpin	Frank J. Pazdera
Philip S. Baldwin	Donald E. Hardy	C. J. C. Quinn
Julius H. Barnes	Dorothy Hartigan	Jugh M. Reynolds
Bernard J. L. Beard	Vera Heller	Joseph W. Rice
Sidney Brooks	Frank H. Holden	Gardner Richardson
George Barr Baker	William C. Holzhauer	Edgar Rickard
W. Gordon Brown	Herbert Hoover	John Schuster
Walter Lyman Brown	George F. Howard	Will Shafroth
Edythe M. Callow	Robert A. Jackson	Fred E. Short
Leon J. Cochrane	Elizabeth L. Jarratt	Luigi Sorieri
Edward E. Dailey	Wallace Johnson	R. A. Sawtelle
Joseph W. Dermody	J. W. Krueger	John C. Speaks
Thomas H. Dickinson	S. Grace Little	Lewis L. Strauss
H. H. Fisher	James A. Logan	Robert A. Taft
Edward M. Flesh	John C. Miller	Frederick L. Thompson
Emily Friedland	Mowatt M. Mitchell	Charles E. Thorn
Adaline Fuller	John H. Lange	Patrick S. Verdon
W. Parmer Fuller	Lee C. Morse	Hershel C. Walker
George Inness Gay	John D. Moyer	Joseph Wenderoth
John P. Gregg	Francis J. Murphy	Theodore Whitmarsh
Freda S. Grosser	William R. Nellegar	

POLISH PERSONNEL
1919

Ems Altman	Chas. Eisenberg	W. Puzyna
John Benislawski	Josef Feinstein	Stanislaw Sokolowski
Frances Bernfeld	August Gerber	Illona Suess
Emerich Czapski	Miss Koerner	Stephania Wittenberg
Zofja Czarniecka	Henryk Lobaczwski	Zofia Zaba
Mary deMalhomme	Boleslaw Piekarski	Alexander Znamiecki

SOURCE: Grove, *War's Aftermath*, p. 220.

DOCUMENT NO. 25

PRESIDENT HOOVER *to* ARTHUR S. HENNING, *statement for special*
supplement on Poland for Chicago Tribune, *Paris edition*

April 16, 1929

As I have for many years had the warmest interest in the Polish people,
having witnessed with sympathy their struggles, both during the Armistice
and since, for the establishment of independence and self-government, I
am glad of another occasion to express my happiness in their present prosperity and economic progress, as now evidenced by the forthcoming international exposition at Poznan.

SOURCE: Poland, Misc., Presidential Personal File, HPL.

DOCUMENT NO. 26

Letter, PRESIDENT HOOVER *to* JOHN ROMASZKIEWICZ

August 7, 1930

Mr. John Romaszkiewicz
President, Polish National Alliance
  of the United States of America,
1406 West Division Street
Chicago, Illinois

My dear Mr. Romaszkiewicz:

I am glad to learn of the celebration of the fiftieth anniversary of the
founding of the Polish National Alliance of the United States of North
America, and to express my warm congratulations upon this happy occasion.
The people of Polish blood in this country have brought to this land a devoted
patriotism, high ideals, and a wide variety of talents which have rendered
splendid service. The Polish National Alliance has been especially useful
in educational, welfare and other community enterprises looking to human
advancement. I wish for its members every success in the continuance of
these important labors.

Yours faithfully,
HERBERT HOOVER

SOURCE: Poland, Misc., Presidential Personal File, HPL.

DOCUMENT NO. 27

*Message from President Hoover read at the unveiling ceremonies
of the monument to President Wilson at Poznan*

July 4, 1931

Despite the distances of space and the differences of speech which separate Poland and the United States, there are circumstances which make it natural for me to express an especial interest in this ceremony. It has been my own good fortune to visit Poland. It has been my good fortune to meet the illustrious citizen of Poland to whose inspiration this gathering is due. It has been my good fortune to know President Wilson, to whom it was given to play a part in the history of Poland. In so doing he cannot have been forgetful of another stormy moment of the world's affairs, when Kosciuszko, Pulaski, and other Polish volunteers, making their way across seas so much wider and more untravelled than they are now, fought in the ragged regiments of Washington. The intervening century and a half have renewed and multiplied past all count these old relations between the people of our two countries. It is therefore peculiarly touching to us that a ceremony such as this should take place in Poland, on the anniversary which stands first in our calendar. In the name of the people of the United States, as in my own, I wish to give voice to our profound appreciation of so notable a mark of remembrance, sympathy, and friendliness.

SOURCE: Public Statements, HPL.

DOCUMENT NO. 28

*President Hoover's remarks made at formal presentation at White House of
credentials of new ambassador of Poland, Tytus Filipowicz*

March 4, 1930

Mr. Ambassador:

It is a source of deep gratification to me that the Government of the Republic of Poland has testified to its good will and friendship for the United States by raising its diplomatic mission at this capital to the rank of an Embassy. It affords me particular pleasure to receive, as I now am happy to do, as the first accredited Ambassador Extraordinary and Plenipotentiary of Poland to the United States, one who, in his former capacity of Envoy

Extraordinary and Minister Plenipotentiary, has given abundant evidence of his cordial personal good will and who has entirely won our esteem.

The American people, who have viewed with friendly interest and sympathy the rapid development of the Polish State, have expressed their warm approval of the action of this Government in raising to the rank of an Embassy its diplomatic mission at Warsaw. In this action, and in the responsive action of your Government, I believe may be found a complete confirmation of the wish of the United States and Poland to maintain with one another the closest and most cordial relations.

I am deeply appreciative of the friendly sentiments which you have expressed to me. I am glad to avail myself of this opportunity to extend to you my best wishes for the continued success of your mission in the United States.

SOURCE: Public Statements, HPL.

DOCUMENT NO. 29

Hoover address delivered on Puɫaski Memorial Day

New York, October 11, 1939
THE SPIRIT OF POLAND

. . . The Polish people more than a thousand years ago settled on the plains between the two great military races of Germany and Russia. They have been overrun time and again. They have been partitioned time and again. But just as often they have fought for their freedom. And the indomitable spirit of the race has time and again led them out of oppression into independence.

I saw something of Poland even before the Great War. Then she was under the heel of Russia, Austria, and Germany. Her commerce and industry were restricted. Her people was exploited. A depressing poverty was her fate. It was the most backward part of all Europe. She held her religious faith only by struggle. Freedom of speech, of press, or even language was repressed. Poles were not allowed in even trivial offices of government. They were driven by ruthless military organization of foreigners. Poland's only intellectual outlet was in art and literature and music. Into these she poured her genius generously to the whole world. Her exiled sons fought for the freedom of others. As did Pulaski and Kosciuszko. Their service in our fight for independence has had a never-ending gratitude from our people.

Soon after the Armistice in 1918 I represented the American Government in such cooperation as we were able to give to the distinguished leaders of

Poland in the erection of the new Polish state. I have had the honor of intimate association with Pilsudski, with Paderewski, and with their many
other able leaders in the rebuilding of an independent government.

I knew as few Americans could know the gigantic task which faced those
men and the Polish people twenty years ago. To the thousand tasks of sup-
pressed progress imposed by the one hundred and fifty years of oppression
were added four years of incessant trampling and destruction as the battle-
ground between German and Russian armies.

On my return home from that mission in 1920 I had the honor to address
a Polish gathering on the hopes of Poland. In describing that scene at the
time of the Armistice, I said: The occupying armies of Russia, Germany
and Austria had been dissolved into marauding bands. Here was a country
of thirty millions of people in a state of total anarchy. It lay in the midst of
a famine such that the children had ceased to play upon the streets. Thousands of people were dying daily from a raging typhus. Hundreds of thousands of homes had been destroyed. The people were living in the open
fields. A part of the nation was in the terrible grip of new Bolshevik invasion.
The population was incapable of paying taxes. They were without the
means of preserving order or repelling invasion. Their transportation and
communications, already backward, were largely destroyed, and had almost
ceased to function. The people themselves were disintegrated and divided
by one hundred and fifty years of partition. They were without even the
rudimentary experience on which to erect the routine of administrative
government.

They had to undertake to build the whole structure of government with
scarcely a man accustomed to its tasks.

Yet out of the genius of their own race they quickly erected the whole
mechanism of government. An army of half a million was trained and drilled.
The Bolsheviks were driven back to their own lines. A general election was
undertaken under universal franchise. A parliament was set up. Local government was established. They made anew the basis of law and of justice.
A free school system was created. Universities and colleges were opened.
Railways and highways were quickly rebuilt. The mines were opened.

The typhus epidemic was stamped out. Food supplies were organized—
and in half a year the children were again playing in the streets.

Again a little more than a year ago I revisited Poland at the invitation of
the Polish Government and as the guest of the Polish people. I was glad to
accept this invitation, as I had desired to witness the great advance in the
Polish nation under these twenty years of freedom. Here after twenty years
was a nation transformed, regenerated. Slowly perhaps in our terms, the
standards of living were improving. New homes, factories, city buildings
had risen in every city. Transportation and communication were advancing.

The universities had trained the specialists for a nation. Education had become universal. The spirit of a people was daily finding expression in high accomplishment. And in these twenty years the Polish nation under freedom had outdistanced in progress all of the one hundred and fifty years of her previous oppression. That in itself is proof of the undying character and spirit of the Polish nation.

And again today Poland is plunged into the depths by the clash of the same forces. But Poland will not die.

Our immediate task is to do what we can to alleviate the lot of the suffering and the homeless. For that a temporary organization has been created to do what it can. With them are leading Americans of Polish descent. That body merits your generous support.

We have the faith that some day a new Poland will rise again. We know the freedom and independence of no great people can be destroyed. Oppression is one of the forces which regenerates the oppressed and destroys the oppressor. No matter what may be signed on papers called peace, there can be no permanent stability and no permanent peace to either Germany or Russia so long as oppression of a great and independent race continues. We know that a people who have fought for a thousand years, who have lost and won again, will not die.

SOURCE: Herbert Hoover, *Further Addresses upon the American Road, 1938–1940* (New York: Charles Scribner's Sons, 1940), pp. 227–30.

DOCUMENT NO. 30

Hoover address at mass meeting in the Chicago Stadium under auspices of the Polish-American Council

Chicago, February 10, 1940

POLISH RELIEF

. . . My part tonight is to discuss an immediate task. We are faced today with a gigantic task of alleviating the sufferings of the people of Poland. There are destruction and suffering in Poland that I could not adequately portray even if I wished to do so. Millions of people must have food; they must have clothing; they must have shelter. Whatever can be done by public charity must be done. But before the next harvest imports of food from abroad on a large scale must be found. It may cost as much as $20,000,000. Charity can be of great aid, but starvation can be prevented only by the cooperation of governments.

With a view to securing this cooperation I joined last fall in organizing the Commission for Relief in Poland. Its primary purpose was to serve the people of German-occupied Poland. In it I called back the men who have served Poland in 1919. It has the presidency of Mr. McCormick and the direction of Maurice Pate, who give their all as volunteers in a great cause, who know the problem.

I am anxious at this critical time that this problem should be understood by you to whom it is so vital. In order for it to succeed the following conditions must be met:

First: Supplies to German-occupied Poland must pass the British blockade. The British must be guaranteed that these supplies are going to the Polish people and not to their enemy.

Second: Any supplies must be transported over German territory and the German authorities must cooperate to secure transportation and freedom from tariffs and charges.

Third: There must be finance with which to buy supplies. In that the British, French, Polish and American governments are the only likely participants.

Fourth: Ships carrying these supplies must have immunities from attack by both belligerents.

Fifth: Supplies must be bought on a large scale and regular shipping must be secured to transport them.

Sixth: The distribution in Poland must be supervised by an American or other neutral staff. These must be men of the highest integrity and devotion. And they must be trained in this work. They must be allowed to move freely in Poland and other countries. They must be neutral in every action, for they have responsibilities to belligerents upon both sides of the war. This supervising staff is necessary to assure just distribution of relief without regard to race or creed. And this supervision is a *sine qua non* also as a guarantee that the relief reaches only the Polish population. Otherwise there can be no hope of securing passage through the blockade or securing finance and support from governments or voluntary committees.

The first step of these negotiations has been taken up the agreements needed. [*sic*] There have been great delays. But we are hopeful that we shall succeed. If we fail it will be from no fault on our side.

The second step was to negotiate with the British, French and Polish governments. This implies not only freedom to move food and staff but aid in finance. Those questions cannot however be settled until the agreement is reached with the Germans. I had hoped I could announce to you tonight that these negotiations were completed. But it is yet delayed.

In the meantime there are hundreds of thousands of Polish refugees outside of Poland. That task must also be served. The Commission for Relief in

Poland has aided in organizing this work. But the time has come when the two tasks should be divided into definitely separate organizations. And support must now be more vigorously organized on their behalf pending the solution of organization in Poland itself.

There is one phase of the relief of suffering abroad to which I wish to refer tonight. Propaganda has been put in motion in the country protesting against American aid to people outside our own borders. Some of it is most genuine anxiety that there shall be no deprival of our own unemployed. Much of it is based on the sound thought that charity begins at home.

A considerable part of it, however, is organized Communistic and other subversive propaganda. So far as the Communistic propaganda is concerned, the kind of people who kill women and children by dropping bombs on them every day would naturally wish to starve them also.

I do wish, however, to answer the question on its merits to those who are sincerely anxious on this question. At the outset I may say that I have repeatedly stated that we do not want a single contribution or any action by our government that would deprive our fellow-countrymen of any need. Americans can never allow our fellow citizens to go hungry or cold.

There are many answers that might be given to the idea that we should give nothing to the war-distressed in Europe. The most important answer is that we are sending commodities produced by our own labor and farmers and that we in our country have a surplus of every single commodity or of every single thing that these people abroad are in need of. Or we could produce such a surplus any time it was called for. Ours is not a country destitute of the materials out of which our people can live, as are these other countries. If all the needs of our people were met tomorrow, we could still produce a surplus of the things that would save the lives of these people abroad. Such destitution as we have in America comes from faulty economic organization, from which flow large unemployment and difficulties to our farmers. That indeed must be remedied. The debate on how that can be done would take me quickly into politics and there should be no politics in relief of human suffering, whether at home or abroad. In the meantime, we have effective agencies in every part of the United States which can and will prevent hunger and cold to our people. These agencies are supported by the taxpayer and by scores of charitable agencies. There should be no restriction on any legitimate expenditure to this end. We are indeed today spending nearly four billion dollars per annum on relief of destitution in the United States. The sums which we are talking about to save people abroad from actual death and starvation and suffering are infinitesimal compared to this four billion. I presume all the need we are looking for for the next six months could be covered with one-half of one per cent of that which we are spending on our own unemployment. America is still rich enough to stretch another one-half per cent. And I do believe that the American people earnestly wish that we as a Christian people and as a free people should not stand by with a surplus of food and see other people in the world die for want of it.

I am connected with another fund; I have been proud of that fund in that we have received subscriptions from over one million of people in less amounts than five dollars. Moreover that fund has been vigorously supported by American labor from one end of the country to the other. The external expression of charity from workers towards workers has not been dimmed, for those who have the least know most of what suffering means. And it is in their giving that comes real sacrifice and it is from them that comes real sympathy for hardship.

Oppression is one of those forces which regenerate the oppressed and destroy the oppressor. No matter what may be signed on papers called peace, there will be no permanent stability and no permanent peace in the world so long as oppression of a great and independent race continues.

In the meantime, our duty is clear. That is to alleviate the suffering of Poland.

SOURCE: "Mass Meeting in the Chicago Stadium under Auspices of the Polish-American Council," Public Statements, HPL.

DOCUMENT NO. 31

Hoover statement to House Foreign Affairs Committee

February 29, 1940

MR. HOOVER: Mr. Chairman and gentlemen of the committee, I was honored to receive the invitation of the committee to appear in support of the legislation providing foodstuffs for Poland. There are probably many detailed questions that would occur to you and I might be of aid to the committee, and I will be glad to do anything I can in that regard.

The situation in Poland in a large sense is familiar to you from the evidence already before you. It may be summarized in a few sentences: Poland has now been dismembered into three segments, the one on the east, in the possession of Russia; and the one on the west incorporated in the German Reich; with a regime established in between which we may call central Poland.

The Poles are normally a self-supporting people in food. This dismemberment, however, has taken the surplus food producing areas away from the central section. The section that has been taken over by Russia normally produces a surplus. But that surplus is now in the possession of the Russians.

There is normally some surplus in production beyond the domestic needs in that section which has been taken over and incorporated in the Reich.

The central section which, as I said, has been established as a special government, normally imports from the other two areas. This central section has a normal population of probably 12 or 13 million and there has been a wholesale transfer into it of Poles and Jews from the section taken over by the Reich and some migration from the section taken over by Russia. The Russians have expropriated most of the agricultural lands in their section to the Government and the result has been a considerable migration of Poles from the Russian-occupied area over into Central Poland. So probably the population there now is somewhere around 13 to 14 million and it is probably growing.

We have very little statistical evidence as to what the food necessities are. Our estimates are based on somewhat theoretical calculations and a sort of a summary of such incidental evidence as we can obtain from people who are traveling back and forth. Theoretically the central area has its own food supply to support probably seven or eight million out of that thirteen or fourteen million people that are now in that area. The last harvest is largely consumed. No doubt there will be an acute food shortage beginning some time in the early spring, lasting until the harvest. Exactly how many people will have to be fed is always a matter of doubt. It seems that at least seven million will have to have some supplementary food supply. A theoretical calculation would imply a very large cost. The mass feeding of human beings is not to be envisaged in terms of grocery bills. As a matter of fact, if we are compelled to reduce the living standards of a people to the very minimum on which the human animal can exist the cost of support per capita per month is not as great as people ordinarily estimate. Theoretically one bushel of wheat and three pounds of fats will keep human beings alive on a sort of animal basis. That is a cost of probably a dollar or $1.75 a month. I am not advocating that. But when calculating the cost of saving a population from actual death and destruction by starvation we are not dealing with the kind of living standards we are accustomed to in the United States. Even the most drastic regime would require supplemental foodstuffs to protect the health of women and children.

All together, by drastic calculations we arrive at a rough calculation of 40 or 50 million dollars to carry the Poles over for another twelve months. We are not suggesting that all that burden fall on the United States. There are other Governments who are interested and are willing to contribute. I have no doubt that somewhere between ten and twenty million dollars would represent a fair share from the United States.

The problems of relief on a wholesale scale under war conditions are not at all simply problems of food. There are military questions of the first order.

Relief not only has to be financed on a large scale but there must be an agreement with the belligerents on all sides for protection. The allied powers will not permit food supplies to pass the blockade into Poland without guarantees that such food supplies will be consumed by the civil population of Poland. Americans are naturally not willing that food supplies at our cost shall be distributed in Poland unless they are distributed with justice to all races and to all parts of the population. The Germans are insistent that any group engaged in operations of this kind shall be completely neutral in their attitudes and not be engaged directly or indirectly in enterprises that might be objectionable to the German cause. It was found in the last war that if populations who are in such a plight as the Poles are to be saved from sheer starvation some sort of organized trusteeship that is agreeable to all of the nations concerned will have to be erected. Such organization will also need undertake the transportation and the distribution in addition to the guarantees to the combatants on both sides.

In an effort to at least make a start in that direction, and at the request of the Polish authorities, I last October summoned a meeting of the Americans who had been engaged in the relief of Poland in the year 1919–20. I requested that they undertake preliminary steps toward setting up such an organization. They established themselves under the title of the Commission for Relief in Poland. Certain of their members were sent to Europe. With the aid of our diplomatic representatives they conducted negotiations with the German, with the British, with the French, and with the fugitive Polish Governments. They have made some progress in the multiple agreements that are necessary. They have had some assurance of financial support from the different governments. These negotiations are not complete. There is some difference of view as between the allied governments and the German Government as to what the character of supervision should be to be set up for the distribution of food in Poland. Those negotiations are progressing and there is every reason to hope that they can be carried through. While I am not able to state that a basis of agreement has been arrived at with the British on one side and the Germans on the other by which such a trustee body can be erected, yet I have hopes it will be carried through in the course of the next few weeks.

It is of very little importance as to what individuals comprise the commission entrusted with these relations with the different nations involved. There are very few men who want to undertake that kind of responsibility for service without pay. I want no misunderstanding that the group of men who were represented yesterday by Mr. McCormick before your committee are at all anxious to undertake this. Any organization that will be agreeable to the many governments involved will be greatly welcomed by those gentlemen.

I believe that in legislation of this sort it would be desirable to provide that the President determine what organization should be set up. It would of course need to be set up in cooperation with some four or five different Governments. . . .

SOURCE: Public Statements, HPL.

DOCUMENT NO. 32

Extracts from Hoover address at Madison Square Garden mass meeting under auspices of the Polish National Council of New York

New York, March 12, 1940

RELIEF FOR POLAND

My part tonight is to discuss an immediate task. And I have rather an important announcement to make to you a little later on.

We are faced today with the necessity of an immediate food supply to something from seven to ten millions of people in Poland. I am anxious at this critical time that the problems of this relief should be understood by you to whom it is so vital. And in order that so gigantic a task should succeed certain foundations must be laid for it.

We have two quite different problems. There is medical and hospital supplies which the American Red Cross generously supplies. Beyond that is the far larger and more difficult problem of food supply for seven million people. That problem comes entirely outside the scope of the American Red Cross. That means hundreds of thousands of tons of foodstuffs. It means during the next few months the finding of fifty millions of dollars. It involves military questions of blockade and supervision which do not apply to medical supplies alone. It implies finance not alone by charity but by government.

It was in realization that these larger problems would arise that the Polish Ambassador asked me some time last fall to interest myself in the solution of these much larger problems. I in turn remobilized the men who had part of the relief of Poland twenty years ago to associate themselves to undertake these difficult negotiations. Under Mr. McCormick, Mr. Pate and some ten or twelve of the men who gave their devoted service in 1919 they have started a temporary organization with view to solution of the many complicated problems with which we are confronted. They have carried on these negotiations unceasingly with Paris, Berlin, in London and Washington during the past four months.

To accomplish this an administrative organization must be set up which has the ability to buy or receive large amounts of foodstuffs. It must have warehouses in a dozen places in the world.

That organization must have agreement from the British, and the French governments to pass those cargo ships through the blockade.

It must have agreement with the German government that these ships will be free of submarine attack and that facilities will be given for inland transportation and that there will be freedom from tariffs and taxes.

And there must be provision for financial support by the British and French governments and from the exiled Polish government. They should have an appropriation of food supplies from our American surplus by the American government.

Now in order to assure the Allied governments and all the donors of these funds that these foodstuffs shall be used solely for the civil populations and that there shall be a just distribution among the population of every race and faith in Poland, there must be a supervision by an adequate American staff.

Furthermore, there can only be one food-shipping and distributing agency. That is a necessity by the nature of the problem. That agency must receive and act for all the different charitable organizations and governmental agencies. . . .

Now I am happy to tell you that within the last twenty-four hours the first step in this negotiation has been consummated. It is now agreed that relief shipments on this great scale shall be free from attack on both sides from both belligerents. It is agreed that distribution shall be set up entirely and conducted in Poland under American hands. We are now in position to start food toward Poland at once. And as a matter of fact it will begin to start this week.

Now the second great problem in the building up of an assurance of living to these millions of people is finance. We are in hopes that the American government will join in this great task. Members of the Congress of both parties have proposed that our government appropriate a part of our surplus of farm products to this great and humane effort.

In the meantime whatever can be provided by charity will be a saving of human life and suffering, and should be provided at once. . . .

As a God-fearing nation or as a liberty-loving nation we have no moral right to stand by with these huge surpluses of food and see people starve who are helpless to help themselves. . . .

We have had a series of criticisms that have arisen that seem to mean that we are to violate neutrality somewhere by some of these operations. The immediate answer to that is that if we enter we do so with the approval by agreement of both combatants and so keep out of range of war. But there is a greater answer than technical explanations. When the greatest Teacher of mankind discussed the action of the Samaritan he did not discuss the question of neutrality. Neither in fact or in spirit is the saving of human life or suffering a violation of neutrality, either now or in any time in history.

SOURCE: "Relief for Poland, Madison Square Garden Mass Meeting under Auspices of the Polish National Council of New York," Public Statements, HPL.

DOCUMENT NO. 33

Telegram, HOOVER *to* MAURICE PATE [*Paderewski Eulogy*]

June 1941

Maurice Pate
Hyannis, Massachusetts

Will you convey the following message to Mr. Paderewski's friends.

Mr. Paderewski's passing brings grief to millions of people. Even his quality as an artist was transcended by his ability as a spiritual leader and statesman. His leadership in the restoration of Polish independence, in the establishment of the reunited nation will live for all time in Polish history. And in the later years of his life, although ill and feeble, when the Poles were again enslaved, he again was the spiritual leader for their freedom.

To those of us who worked with him in these matters over the years, the passing of his leadership is a great loss. But his inspiration will ever continue.

HERBERT HOOVER

SOURCE: Maurice Pate, Post-Presidential Papers, HPL.

DOCUMENT NO. 34

Extracts from Hoover article appearing in Collier's, *April 27, 1940*

RUSSIAN MISADVENTURE

. . . I propose to analyze Mr. Roosevelt's recognition of the Communist government of Soviet Russia and its consequences to the American people and to mankind. . . .

On August 23, 1939, the world was startled by an alliance of Fascist Hitler and Communist Stalin. This was no surprise to thinking people to whom the blood brotherhood was well known. It was embarrassing to a vast number of pseudo-liberals who had tried to envisage Fascism as the sole living devil of civilization.

Nine days after this junction these governments simultaneously attacked independent Poland. They destroyed the freedom of a great people. . . . On November 30th last came the unprovoked attack by Russia upon little Finland. Here the might of 160 million Russians was thrown against 3.5 million peace loving and liberty loving Finns. . . .

As a sop for the recognition, an appeal was made to the cupidity of the American people. We were told in 1933 that upon this recognition Russia would buy a vast amount of American goods. A good part of American business was brought to support recognition by large promises of new business.

. . . In the five months since Poland was attacked our sales of goods to Russia have increased 300%. This represents a large addition of gasoline, copper, alloys, etc. to aid in the subjugation of the liberties of the Finns and the Poles and other peoples.

SOURCE: Herbert Hoover, *Further Addresses,* pp. 158–71.

DOCUMENT NO. 35

Hoover address delivered in Warsaw, Poland

Warsaw, March 30, 1946
ON THE FOOD SITUATION IN POLAND

This is the worst situation we have seen so far in every respect. It is lightened only by the hope and gallantry of the Polish people. They are digging themselves out of the greatest physical, political, intellectual and moral destruction ever known. But my Mission has no part in political, economic or social matters. It is solely concerned with food.

Armies have four times swept over Poland, living on the country, and she had five years of German occupation. The population of new Poland, about twenty-four million, will be about eleven million less than old Poland, of which probably 5,000,000 were killed. A Polish woman remarked to me today, "We are weary of dying."

There has been enormous destruction of housing, amounting to 90 per cent in Warsaw alone. Most of the people in the destroyed areas are living in hovels without adequate clothing, furniture, or heat.

Compared to pre-war, the horses remaining are stated to be only 45 per cent; cattle, 33 per cent; sheep, 36 per cent; swine, 17 per cent; and they are mostly underfed. But of even more importance has been the intellectual destruction and physical weakening of the human beings.

The food situation has become sudden and heartbreaking due to mis-calculations. The breadstuffs and potatoes in stock and enroute from over-seas will theoretically last only until May 7th on a reduced ration. The bread ration is a theoretical average of seven ounces per day per person, and two cities, Crakow and Lodz, have already been without bread for three weeks at a time. The fat ration, when you can get it, is 16 ounces per month per person. The average caloric intake, including hospital inmates, is perhaps 1,500 (mostly starches), but inability to create effective distribution makes any estimate unreliable. Examination by American experts shows over 2,500,000 children are estimated to be terribly sub-normal from under-nourishment. Dairy products are practically unknown to the great majority of city children. Samplings indicate an infant mortality of 20 per cent per annum, with a huge increase of tuberculosis and other under-feeding diseases among all children and adolescents. There are 1,100,000 orphans and half-orphans. Five million children should have more food and more appropriate food at once. Children cannot wait for their reconstruction until some other time; their future is being made now. Unlike after the first World War, there has been no over-all organization to care for and rebuild the children. There are gallant efforts by Polish women in local areas, con-ducted under unbelievable difficulty. They are receiving some assistance from the American Red Cross and the American Catholic Welfare.

Added to all the other problems is the migration of some millions of Poles westward from the territory annexed by Russia, and the expulsion of Germans west from the territory annexed by Poland. Both migrations add to the already disorganized food situation.

It is a forbidding picture, but, with food until the next harvest, Poland can rise again from her ashes.

SOURCE: Herbert Hoover, *Addresses upon the American Road by Herbert Hoover, 1945–1948* (New York: D. Van Nostrand Co., 1949), pp. 183–84.

DOCUMENT NO. 36

Statement by Herbert Hoover for The Polish Review

November 19, 1949

The Polish Nation was betrayed not only by the Germans but by the Russians, and also by the Western Allies, who defaulted on the Atlantic Charter which had been held out as the faith and hope for all peoples.

The Polish Nation has fought for its independence and the freedom of its people for over 1000 years. It has often succeeded, only to be eclipsed by the aggression of its neighbors for long periods. That spirit in the Polish race cannot be submerged forever. There lie in this Nation those inspirations for freedom and independence that will yet carry it to independence and freedom.

SOURCE: Poland, Post-Presidential Papers, HPL.

DOCUMENT NO. 37

Message of Herbert Hoover read over Radio Free Europe on the 162nd anniversary of the Polish Constitution

May 3, 1953

I have been both happy and unhappy about the condition of the Polish people many times during the past forty years. I saw Poland in 1913, when she was suffering from one hundred fifty years of partition. I saw her in 1919 when her independence was restored. I saw her in 1938 after twenty years of freedom. I witnessed her marvelous growth under the impulses of free men. And I saw her again in 1946 under the heel of Communist oppression.

The Polish people for more than a thousand years have suffered under repeated subjugation. But the indomitable spirit of the race has time and again led them out of oppression into freedom.

The spirit of a great race does not die from oppression. A free Poland is not dead. It will rise again; and its people will once more live according to the spirit and the principles of its noble Constitution of 1791—the anniversary of which you are celebrating in your hearts today.

There is more to nations than their soil, their cities, their wealth, and even their government. There is a soul in a great people. That soul is forged in the instincts of their race, their traditions, their heroic struggle, their heroic men, and their genius in art, music and literature. It is steeled in their sufferings. They may be impoverished. But the soul of a great people cannot be crushed. From that their national life and their freedom will rise again and again from the ashes of their homes.

HERBERT HOOVER

SOURCE: Dolbeare, Post-Presidential Individual Files, HPL.

Notes to Introductory Essay

1. Stetson to Hoover, November 15, 1928, Stetson, Pre-Presidential Papers, Hoover Presidential Library, West Branch, Iowa (hereafter cited as HPL).

2. Hoover to Walter S. Heebner, November 10, 1963, Post-Presidential Personal Correspondence, HPL. Whatever the exact date of their first meeting in the early 1890s in California, Hoover gave a slightly different account in *The Memoirs of Herbert Hoover: Years of Adventure, 1874–1920* (New York: Macmillan Co., 1952), p. 357.

3. Harold Henry Fisher and Sidney Brooks, *America and the New Poland* (New York: Macmillan Co., 1928), p. 84. In September 1926 Hoover had discussed with Fisher the need for a scholarly book, not only covering the A.R.A.'s years in Poland, but also providing a general account of Polish-American relations. When Fisher's book was published, Hoover wrote to him: "I wish to express my admiration for your book. . . . It is a good job and I feel greatly complimented by it personally." (Hoover to Fisher, April 13, 1928, Commerce Papers, HPL.)

4. Fisher and Brooks, *America and the New Poland,* pp. 90–91.

5. "Résumé of American Relief Operations in Europe 1918–1920," Hoover to Alexander Loveday, January 18, 1943, in Suda Lorena Bane and Ralph Haswell Lutz, eds., *Organizations of American Relief in Europe, 1918–1919* (Stanford: Stanford University Press, 1943), pp. 2–3.

6. In Bane and Lutz, *Organization of American Relief,* p. 67.

7. William R. Grove, *War's Aftermath (Polish Relief in 1919)* (New York: House of Field, 1940), pp. 28–29.

8. Ibid., p. 35.

9. Alvin Barton Barber, "Hoover's Aid to Poland," Poland, Pre-Presidential Correspondence, HPL.

10. Quoted in Fisher and Brooks, *America and the New Poland,* p. 179; see also Grove, *War's Aftermath,* p. 36.

11. Hoover, *Memoirs,* pp. 356–57. Vernon Kellogg gives no indication of these events either in his *Herbert Hoover: The Man and His Work* (New York: D. Appleton & Co., 1920) or in his "Preliminary Report on Conditions in Poland," published in *Organization of American Relief,* eds. Bane and Lutz, pp. 150–58. While giving an interesting account of what he called "a little operabouffe coup d'état" (January 4–5, 1919), Kellogg stressed that "we are being very careful to keep free from political matters and discussion." Nowhere does he indicate asking for or receiving Hoover's authorization to submit a political ultimatum to Piłsudski. Hoover's version is corroborated by Wilson's claim at one of the Peace Conference

meetings in Paris on May 17, 1919, that Paderewski had in his possession a letter from Hoover, endorsed by the president, which stated that American aid to Poland was dependent upon Paderewski's being prime minister. The date of that communication, however, was not given by Wilson. (See U.S., Department of State, *Papers Relating to Foreign Relations of the United States: Paris Peace Conference 1919* [Washington, D.C.: Government Printing Office, 1942], 5: 676.) Two authors, Samuel L. Sharp in *Poland: White Eagle on a Red Field* (Cambridge, Mass.: Harvard University Press, 1953), pp. 77, 114, and Louis Gerson in *Woodrow Wilson and the Rebirth of Poland* (New Haven: Yale University Press, 1953), p. 107, accept Hoover's version without reservation. Two Polish scholars, Titus Komarnicki in *Rebirth of the Polish Republic: A Study in the Diplomatic History of Europe, 1914– 1920* (London: William Heinemann, 1957), p. 261, and Piotr S. Wandycz in *France and Her Eastern Allies, 1919–1925* (Minneapolis: University of Minnesota Press, 1962), p. 20, argue for an opposite point of view, blaming Hoover for a memory failure (Komarnicki) or blaming Gerson for "many misconceptions and factual mistakes" (Wandycz). Conclusive documentary proof for either position is missing.

12. Poland, American Relief Administration (hereafter cited as Poland, A.R.A.) (London), Hoover Institution Archives, Stanford, Calif. (hereafter cited as HIA); for full text see Document 15.

13. Roman Dębicki, *Foreign Policy of Poland, 1919–1939: From the Rebirth of the Polish Republic to World War II* (New York: Frederick A. Praeger, 1962), p. 12.

14. Ronald Emil Swerczak, *The Diplomatic Career of Hugh Gibson 1908– 1938,* microfilm (Ph.D. diss., University of Iowa, 1972), pp. 113–14.

15. Grove, *War's Aftermath,* pp. 36–37.

16. In Bane and Lutz, *Organization of American Relief,* p. 152.

17. Hoover to General Andrews (cable), January 31, 1919, Poland, A.R.A. (Paris), HIA.

18. Grove, *War's Aftermath,* p. 100.

19. Ibid.

20. "Memorandum on Sir John Beale's Note of February 5th in Respect to my Preliminary Programmes to Liberated Countries Presented February 3rd," A.R.A., HIA.

21. Fisher and Brooks, *America and the New Poland,* p. 176.

22. Hoover to Edouard Beneš, March 11, 1919, in Bane and Lutz, *Organization of American Relief,* p. 329. See Bane and Lutz, pp. 293–98, for the bilateral agreements.

23. Hoover to Wilson, April 2, 1919, in Fisher and Brooks, *America and the New Poland,* p. 169. The authors give examples of German attempts to "test the powers of Article 16 of the Armistice" with regard to the Polish use of the port of Gdańsk, actions for which the Germans were sharply rebuked, first by Maj. James W. Webb, chief of the operations in that port city, and then by Hoover's Food Section of the Supreme Economic Council with a warning that "the Germans . . . must conform with the letter and spirit of Article 16" (pp. 169–71).

24. In Bane and Lutz, *Organization of American Relief,* p. 425.

25. Fisher and Brooks, *America and the New Poland,* p. 202.

26. Hoover to Goodyear, May 2, 1919, in Bane and Lutz, *Organization of American Relief,* pp. 454 – 55. See also Goodyear to Paderewski, May 8, 1919, in

Halina Janowska and Czesław Madajczyk, eds., *Archiwum polityczne Ignacego Paderewskiego* (Wrocław: Ossolineum, 1974), 2: 147–48.

27. Fisher and Brooks, *America and the New Poland,* p. 206.

28. Ibid., p. 207.

29. Ibid., pp. 207–8.

30. See Anson C. Goodyear's "Report of the Coal Commission for the Territory Included in the Former Empire of Austria-Hungary and Poland," in Bane and Lutz, *Organization of American Relief,* pp. 686–713.

31. Fisher and Brooks, *America and the New Poland,* p. 198.

32. In Janowska and Madajczyk, *Archiwum polityczne,* 2: 141.

33. See Bernard D. Weinryb, *The Jews of Poland: A Social and Economic History of the Jewish Community in Poland from 1100 to 1800* (Philadelphia: Jewish Publication Society of America, 1973), and Simon Dubnow, *History of the Jews in Russia and Poland,* vol. 1 (Philadelphia: Jewish Publication Society of America, 1946).

34. Fisher and Brooks, *America and the New Poland,* p. 156. To support their view, the authors quote the report of the Viennese *Neue Freie Presse* (November 30, 1918) that the number of Jewish victims in Lwów was between 2,500 and 3,000, whereas the local Jewish authorities of Lwów put the maximum at 76 (p. 156). A similar opinion about exaggerations and the absence of official Polish complicity in the killing of "some Jews" in Pińsk for "suspected collaboration with the Bolsheviks" was expressed by Hugh Gibson. He mentioned, however, Marshal Piłsudski's acknowledgment that "the antisemitic persecution had occured." Piłsudski (never anti-Semitic himself) confirmed "the revival of terrorism, including the forcibly cutting off beards of Jews." (Swerczak, *Diplomatic Career of Hugh Gibson,* p. 125–26.)

35. Swerczak, *Diplomatic Career of Hugh Gibson,* pp. 128–31, 161. For his alleged partiality to the Polish point of view and apologies for the Paderewski government, Gibson was criticized as an anti-Semite by the president of the American Jewish Committee, Louis Marshall. He was defended, however, by another Jewish notable, Abraham I. Elkys, the former U.S. ambassador to Turkey, who upon being shown Gibson's dispatches to the State Department told Polk that he was entirely satisfied and had "utmost confidence in Gibson." (Ibid.)

36. Fisher and Brooks, *America and the New Poland,* p. 157. Hoover's intervention is favorably discussed in Herman Bernstein's article in the September 1925 *McClure's.* Excerpts of the article contained in the Lewis Strauss collection among the Pre-Presidential Papers at the Hoover Presidential Library, with a quotation from Strauss to the effect that "the Chief" was always fair to the Jews. Paderewski's cooperation in that delicate matter obviously satisfied Hoover since he mentioned in his March 9, 1921, cable to F. L. Polk: "I was perhaps more intimately in contact with him . . . in the first few months of the reestablishment of the independence of that nation than any other American. I know that . . . he developed full protection to the helpless element . . . particularly the Jews, and laid the foundation for relationship among the people that must be tolerant and enduring." (Janowska and Madajczyk, *Archiwum polityczne,* 2: 632–33.)

37. "The Morgenthau Report" in *Jews in Poland: Official Reports of the American and British Investigating Missions* (Chicago: National Polish Committee of America, 1920), pp. 4–9. For an argument between Hoover and Felix Frankfurter over the fact-finding missions, see the latter's *Reminiscences: Recorded in Talks with Dr. Harlan B. Phillips* (New York: Reynal & Co., 1960), pp. 156–57.

38. "The Jadwin and Johnson Report," in *Jews in Poland,* pp. 11–17. The reports of the mission were submitted by President Wilson and Secretary Lansing to both houses of Congress in mid-January 1920 and published as Senate Document 177, 66th Cong., 2d sess.

39. Hoover to Parker, June 21, 1919, in Bane and Lutz, *Organization of American Relief,* p. 559.

40. Gilchrist, "The American Typhus Relief Expedition to Poland," *A.R.A. Bulletin* (Paris), ser. 1, vol. 3, no. 20 (August 1, 1919):1–5, HIA; Robert A. Taft to W. E. Joyce, September 3, 1919, *A.R.A. Documents, European Operations,* vol. 19, *Poland, Typhus Relief,* mimeographed (Stanford: Stanford University, 1932), p. 447.

41. Hoover to Baker, July 11, 1919, and Baker to Pershing, July 14, 1919, in Bane and Lutz, *Organization of American Relief,* p. 659.

42. Fisher and Brooks, *America and the New Poland,* pp. 245–46.

43. "Report of the American Relief Administration: European Children's Fund Mission to Poland" (Warsaw: A.R.A., 1922), p. 8. HIA.

44. Ibid., p. 9.

45. Ibid., p. 10.

46. Ibid., p. 11.

47. Fisher and Brooks, *America and the New Poland,* p. 217.

48. Grove, *War's Aftermath,* p. 177.

49. Hoover to Grove, Hoover to Baker, Hoover to Pershing, Hoover to Rogers, July 24, 1919, *A.R.A. Documents, European Operations,* 19: 249–54, HIA.

50. Hoover, *Memoirs,* pp. 358–59. According to Hoover's account, it was Wilson who was invited to visit Poland. Since the president could not go, Paderewski urged Hoover to come because the Poles greatly wanted his "advice upon their whole economic situation and upon a further reorganization of the government as soon as possible."

51. Ibid., p. 359. See also Dr. J. Pearce Mitchell's "Carefree Days with Hoover at Campfires," *Palo Alto Times,* August 16, 1964.

52. Kellogg, *Herbert Hoover,* pp. 4–6.

53. Hoover, *Memoirs,* p. 360.

54. For instance, on August 17, 1919, *Gazeta Lwowska* devoted the front page to Hoover's portrait, editorial articles about his visit, reports from his press conference in Warsaw, plus other Hoover information.

55. Hoover, *Memoirs,* p. 360.

56. Hoover to Paderewski, August 17, 1919, in Grove, *War's Aftermath,* pp. 164–67.

57. Hoover to Durand, August 17, 1919, *A.R.A. Documents, European Operations,* 19: 304–5, HIA.

58. Hoover to Gibson (draft), August 17, 1919, Pre-Commerce Papers, HPL (italics in original).

59. "Address of the Hon. Herbert C. Hoover, Palace Hotel, San Francisco, October 1919," HIA. The *San Francisco Chronicle* of October 15 headlined the speech: "Hoover at Commonwealth Club Luncheon Makes Stirring Plea for Aid of European Peoples."

60. Martha Chickering, *Into Free Poland via Germany* (New York: Overseas Department of the YWCA, 1920), p. 5.

61. Barber, "Hoover's Aid to Poland," pp. 10–11. See also the laudatory comments on the A.R.A.'s service to Poland and on the efforts of a Gray Samaritan, Christina Zduleczna, by Coningsby Dawson in *It Might Have Happened to You: A Contemporary Portrait of Central and Eastern Europe* (New York: John Lane Co., 1921), pp. 84–136.

62. Hoover to Lowell, June 26, 1920, Polish Gray Samaritans, HIA.

63. Hoover's letter of August 24, 1922, to the Girls of the Gray Samaritan, Unit of the Y.W.C.A., HIA. Hoover also mentions that Polish-American unit in his article "How Much Longer Must We Feed Europe," *Forum*, December, 1920.

64. Fuller, "Bolshevism, Food, and Other Troubles," January 22, 1920, Poland, A.R.A. (London), HIA.

65. In Komarnicki, *Rebirth of the Polish Republic*, p. 682. The author is mistaken, by the way, in claiming that Hoover "went twice to Poland during this period in the capacity of Head of the Relief Mission." In fact, between 1914 and 1938 he visited Poland only once, in August 1919.

66. Hoover cable to Warsaw, July 14, 1920, *Poland*, A.R.A. (London), HIA.

67. Frank M. Surface and Raymond L. Bland, *American Food in the World War and Reconstruction Period: Operations of the Organizations under the Direction of Herbert Hoover, 1914–1924* (Stanford: Stanford University Press, 1931), pp. 228–29.

68. Barber, "Hoover's Aid to Poland," p. 13.

69. Ibid.

70. Witos to Hoover, October 29, 1920 (translated), Poland A.R.A., (London), HIA.

71. Herbert Hoover, "Child Life in Central Europe and the Need of Co-operation in Relief," *A.R.A. Bulletin* (Paris) ser. 2, vol. 1, no. 1 (October 1, 1920): 2–3, HIA.

72. "Organization of the Relief Foundation," *A.R.A. Bulletin* (Paris), ser. 2, vol. 2, no. 11 (April 1, 1921): 32, HIA.

73. *Kurjer Lwowski*, Lwów, October 30, 1920 (translated), Poland, A.R.A. (London), HIA.

74. Henryk Bezmaski [Stanisław Posner], "Hoover's Charity Dinner," *Robotnik*, Warsaw, February 13, 1921 (translated), Poland, A.R.A. (London), HIA.

75. Poland, Pre-Presidential Correspondence, HPL.

76. Perrin C. Galpin to Christian A. Herter, December 15, 1921, Commerce Papers, HPL.

77. Hoover to the Children of Kutno, Poland, May 29, 1922. Degrees and Other Honors, Commerce Papers, HPL.

78. Fisher and Brooks, *America and the New Poland*, p. 318.

79. Durand to Hoover, February 24, 1922, Poland, Commerce Papers, HPL.

80. Fisher and Brooks, *America and the New Poland*, p. 319.

81. "For Children in Poland; Action of Herbert Hoover," *Rzeczpospolita* Warsaw, July 4, 1921 (translated), Poland, A.R.A. (London), HIA.

82. Surface and Bland, *American Food*, p. 231.

83. Barber, "Hoover's Aid to Poland," p. 14.

84. Baldwin to Ponikowski, March 1, 1922, A.R.A., HIA.

85. Hoover to Polish Government, April 20, 1922, in Fisher and Brooks, *America and the New Poland*, pp. 361–62.

86. "Proclamation of the President of the Ministers of Poland," in Fisher and Brooks, *America and the New Poland,* pp. 362–63.

87. The only comparable period of American friendship with Poland, particularly among the young intellectuals, occurred in the early 1830s. See Jerzy Jan Lerski, *A Polish Chapter in Jacksonian America* (Madison: University of Wisconsin Press, 1958), pp. 14–33.

88. Gibson to Herter, October 30, 1922, Degrees and Other Honors, Commerce Papers, HPL.

89. Harold H. Fisher, *The Famine in Soviet Russia, 1919–1923: The Operation of the American Relief Administration* (New York: Macmillan Co., 1927), pp. 176–77.

90. Skirmunt to Hoover, August 8, 1921, Poland, A.R.A. (London), HIA.

91. Juliusz Łukasiewicz, *Z doświadczeń przeszłości* [From Past Experiences] (1944), p. 7, quoted by Władysław Pobóg-Malinowski in *Najnowsza historia polityczna Polski, 1864–1945* [Recent Political History of Poland, 1864–1945] (London: 1956), 2: 401.

92. Fisher, *Famine in Soviet Russia,* p. 177.

93. Brown to Baldwin, February 17, 1922, Poland, A.R.A. (London), HIA.

94. Advance press release of April 14, 1928, Individuals—Slavonic Group, Pre-Presidential Campaign Papers, HPL.

95. "Paderewski on Hoover," May 16, 1928, Poland, Pre-Presidential Correspondence, HPL.

96. Walcott to Paderewski, Janowska and Madajczyk, *Archiwum polityczne,* 3: 145.

97. Hoover to Stetson, November 16, 1928, and January 9, 1929, Stetson, Pre-Presidential Papers, HPL.

98. French Strather [Hoover's secretary] to Benjamin T. Anuszkiewicz, April 15, 1929, Presidential Personal File, HPL. A somewhat similar message was sent to Tadeusz Machrowicz for publication in a booklet of the Polish Legion of American Veterans: "The part played by the more than 300,000 Americans of Polish extraction who served in the U.S. Army during the World War was a symbol of the devotion of their compatriots . . . who gave their patriotic zeal and splendid efforts in behalf of the land of their adoption." (Hoover to Machrowicz, July 25, 1932, Presidential Personal File, HPL.)

99. Hoover to Ruszkiewicz, June 12, 1929, Presidential Personal File; Hoover to Mościcki, October 10, 1929, Presidential Personal File, HPL.

100. Hoover to Dominik Gajewski, August 14, 1930, Presidential Personal File, HPL.

101. Hoover to Olejniczak, August 21, 1930, Presidential Personal File, HPL.

102. Ruth Fesler [Hoover's secretary] to Paderewski, November 16, 1930, Janowska and Madajczyk, *Archiwum polityczne,* 3: 176.

103. Aniela Strakacz, *Paderewski as I Knew Him: From the Diary of Aniela Strakacz* (New Brunswick: Rutgers University Press, 1949), p. 111. See also Sylwin Strakacz to Miss Fesler, December 17, 1930, Presidential Personal File, HPL. In February 1932 Hoover planned to attend Paderewski's recital in Baltimore but, prevented from doing so by his doctor due to a cold, he wrote to Paderewski: "I am deeply touched by your thought in having the lovely red roses in the box awaiting me, and am enjoying their loveliness today. My friends, who occupied the box, are

most enthusiastic over the delightful evening you gave your audience in your inimitable way." (Hoover to Paderewski, February 12, 1932, Janowska and Madajczyk, *Archiwum polityczne,* 3: 203.) The roses for the absent Hoover were a sort of reciprocal gesture for the Cadillac presented to Paderewski by Hoover during his premiership in postwar Poland (Strakacz, *Paderewski as I Knew Him,* p. 34).

104. Similarly, in a message to the Federated Polish Cultural Associations of Chicago, the president stressed that "it is indeed fitting that the American citizens of Polish origin should commemorate the ninth anniversary of the death of President Woodrow Wilson, who was their friend . . . and to whose vision and mighty moral power Poland owes much in securing its independent existence with the enjoyment of liberty and the blessings of republican government." (Hoover to Joseph S. Kobrzynski, January 21, 1933, Presidential Personal File, HPL.)

105. "Remarks Made at Formal Presentation at White House of Credentials of New Ambassador of Poland, Tytus Filipowicz," Public Statements, HPL. John N. Willys, one of a number of able career men from the Department of State, was promoted by Hoover to the rank of ambassador to Poland, thus departing from the questionable habit of appointing wealthy campaign contributors. (Ray Lyman Wilbur and Arthur M. Hyde, *The Hoover Policies* [New York: Charles Scribner's Sons, 1937], pp. 585–86.)

106. "Treaty between the United States of America and Poland," signed in Washington June 15, 1931, U.S. Department of State, *Papers Relating to Foreign Relations of the United States, 1931* (Washington D.C.: Government Printing Office, 1946), 2: 938–56 (hereafter cited as *U.S. Foreign Relations*).

107. Robert H. Ferrell, *American Diplomacy in the Great Depression: Hoover– Stimson Foreign Policy, 1929–1933* (New Haver: Yale University Press, 1957), pp. 201–3; Sharp, *Poland,* p. 281.

108. Sharp, *Poland,* p. 280.

109. Claudius O. Johnson, *Borah of Idaho* (New York: Longmans, Green & Co., 1936), p. 447.

110. *U.S. Foreign Relations, 1931,* 1: 603. German historian Werner Link, however, again gave some fuel to anti-Hoover propaganda in Soviet-controlled Poland in his monograph, *Die amerikanische Stabilisierungspolitik in Deutschland, 1921–32* (Düsseldorf: Droste Verlag, 1970), pp. 504–8.

111. *U.S. Foreign Relations, 1931,* 1: 600.

112. Sharp, *Poland,* p. 281.

113. *U.S. Foreign Relations, 1932,* 1: 861–64.

114. Ibid., pp. 279–80.

115. Ibid., pp. 800–807.

116. Wilbur and Hyde, *The Hoover Policies,* pp. 520–23.

117. "Remarks Made at Formal Presentation at White House of Credentials of New Ambassador of Poland, Stanislaus Patek," Public Statements, HPL.

118. Hoover to Samuel M. Vauclain of Baldwin Locomotive Works, October 31, 1932, Presidential Personal File, HPL.

119. Hoover to Leon T. Walkowicz, December 20, 1932, Presidential Personal File, HPL.

120. Harold Wolfe, *Herbert Hoover: Public Servant and Leader of Loyal Opposition* (New York: Exposition Press, 1956), p. 373.

122

121. *Illustrowany Kurier Codzienny,* Kraków, March 13, 1938, and *Y.M.C.A. Bulletin,* n.s. 16, no. 4 (1938), Post-Presidential Papers, HPL.

122. Herbert Hoover, *An American Epic* (Chicago: Henry Regnery Co., 1964), 4: 5–6.

123. "Mr. Hoover Testifies," editorial in *New York Times,* March 3, 1940.

124. "Relief for Poland, Madison Square Garden Mass Meeting under Auspices of the Polish National Council of New York," Public Statements, HPL.

125. "Hoover Says Poles Must Rise Again," *New York Times,* April 29, 1940.

126. "The Paderewski Fund for Polish Relief, Inc., *Campaign Bulletin No. 17,*" April 22, 1940, Poland—Relief, Post-Presidential Papers, HPL.

127. Hoover to Donovan, March 17, 1940, Poland, Post-Presidential Papers, HPL.

128. For instance, in a letter to Witkowski in 1958 Hoover wrote: "I knew [Paderewski] as the greatest of musicians, as a magnificent orator, and as a friend. I am glad you are keeping this great name in history before the American people." And four years later, when awarded a gold medal by the foundation in recognition for his humanitarian work, he wrote: "I regret that because of medical restrictions, I could not attend the festivities last Sunday night. However, as Mr. Pate has shared in all my links with Poland for over forty-five years, it was most fitting that he acted on my behalf. In respect for the friendship and the spirit of Ignacy Jan Paderewski, I am grateful for this tribute. He is a symbol of hope that free Poland will rise again." (Hoover to Witkowski, September 13, 1958, and November 23, 1962, Poland, Post-Presidential Papers, HPL.)

129. Davis—Hoover telephone conversation, March 22, 1940, Poland, Post-Presidential Papers, HPL.

130. Hoover, *An American Epic,* 4: 6–7.

131. Ibid., p. 8.

132. Hon. Jan Ciechanowski, Post-Presidential Individual Files, HPL.

133. Hoover, *An American Epic,* 4: 9.

134. Hoover to Ciechanowski, April 23, 1941, Hon. Jan Ciechanowski, Post-Presidential Individual Files, HPL.

135. Ciechanowski to Hoover, May 14, 1941, Hon. Jan Ciechanowski, Post-Presidential Individual Files, HPL. In the same letter the Polish ambassador had to apologize for indiscretions on the part of the Polish Information Center in New York with regard to Nazi confiscation of Hoover commission foodstuffs in Poland.

136. Undated report, Maurice Pate, Post-Presidential Individual Files, HPL.

137. Herbert Hoover, "Foreign Policies for America," New York City, March 31, 1938, in *Addresses upon the American Road, 1933–1938* (New York: Charles Scribner's Sons, 1938), pp. 317–18.

138. *Saturday Evening Post,* October 27, 1939.

139. "The Nine Horsemen and America," *Liberty Magazine,* June 5, 1940.

140. William L. Langer and S. Everett Gleason, *The Challenge to Isolation: 1937–1940* (New York: Harper & Bros., 1952), p. 479.

141. "Tale of a Girl and a Man Who Should Know," Polish Telegraph Agency (PAT), April 27, 1944, Poland—Relief, Post-Presidential Papers, HPL.

142. Edward J. Rożek, *Allied Wartime Diplomacy: A Pattern in Poland* (New York: John Wiley & Sons, 1958), pp. 300–301.

143. Pate to Hoover, August 9, 1944 (and see Hoover to Pate, August 14, 1944), Maurice Pate, Post-Presidential Individual Files, HPL.

144. His first comment upon hearing the official Yalta communiqué was rather hopeful: "If the agreements' promises and ideals which are expressed shall be carried out, it will open a great hope in the world" (*Chicago Tribune,* February 13, 1945, quoted by Athan G. Theoharis in *The Yalta Myths* [Columbia: University of Missouri Press, 1970], p. 27).

145. Herbert Hoover, "Some Additions to the Dumbarton Oaks Proposals," *Addresses upon the American Road by Herbert Hoover, 1941–1945* (New York: D. Van Nostrand Co., 1946), pp. 111–18.

146. Hoover to Kwapiszewski, July 12, 1945, Kwapiszewski, Post-Presidential Individual Files, HPL.

147. Hoover to Emmet, July 13, 1945, Post-Presidential Papers, HPL.

148. Undated report, Maurice Pate, Post-Presidential Individual Files, HPL.

149. Arthur Bliss Lane, *I Saw Poland Betrayed: An American Ambassador Reports to the American People* (New York: Bobbs-Merrill Co., n.d.), p. 221.

150. Ibid., pp. 221–22.

151. "Remarks at Dinner of President Bierut," March 29, 1946, in *Addresses upon the American Road by Herbert Hoover, 1945–1948* (New York: D. Van Nostrand Co., 1949), pp. 181–82.

152. Lane, *I Saw Poland Betrayed,* p. 222.

153. Ibid., p. 223.

154. Hoover to Byrnes, July 21, 1946, Arthur Bliss Lane, Post-Presidential Individual Files, HPL.

155. Hoover to Mikołajczyk, February 15, 1949, Stanisław Mikołajczyk, Post-Presidential Individual Files, HPL.

156. Hoover to Henry T. Blair, August 4, 1947, Misc., Post-Presidential Papers, HPL.

157. Hoover to Dallin, September 2, 1947, Misc., Post-Presidential Papers, HPL. Individual statements of Polish inmates of Soviet labor camps were collected by General Anders's Second Army Corps after leaving the Soviet Union in 1942. Tens of thousands of these documents were acquired by the Hoover Institution and are available for scholars.

158. Hoover to Walkowicz, August 17, 1949, Poland, Post-Presidential Papers, HPL.

159. Lane to Hoover, August 2, 1950, Arthur Bliss Lane, Post-Presidential Individual Files, HPL.

160. Theoharis, *Yalta Myths,* p. 190.

161. *Addresses upon the American Road, 1950–1955* (Stanford: Stanford University Press, 1955), p. 78.

162. Hoover to Ignatius N. Werwiński, August 5, 1957, Misc., Post-Presidential Papers, HPL.

163. Hoover to Mikołajczyk, October 11, 1956, Poland, Post-Presidential Papers, HPL. As late as August 31, 1964, Hoover was invited to attend the Eighth Congress of the International Peasant Union in Washington, D.C. His secretary answered Mikołajczyk: "Due to his advanced age, Mr. Hoover's doctors are greatly restricting

his activities and it will not be possible for him to attend your meeting. However, I do know that his hopes and prayers are with you as they were in 1956 when he sent a message to the Union." (Naomi Yeager [Hoover's secretary] to Mikołajczyk, n.d., Poland, Post-Presidential Papers, HPL.)

164. Hoover to Dolbeare, April 24, 1953, and Hoover to Egan, November 30, 1955, Poland, Post-Presidential Papers, HPL.

165. *Addresses upon the American Road by Herbert Hoover, 1955–1960* (Caldwell, Idaho: Caxton Printers, 1961), p. 22.

166. Pate to Hoover, March 18, 1957, Maurice Pate, Post-Presidential Individual Files, HPL.

167. *Addresses upon the American Road by Herbert Hoover, 1955–1960,* p. 57.

Index